PRAISE FOR *SOMEBODY SHOULD HAVE TOLD US!*

This book is worth more than a million self-help books. It contains wisdom for a lifetime. It can save a person (and those who know us) from hours of therapy later in life. Jack Pransky gets at the very essence of what drives our happiness. *Somebody Should Have Told Us!* provides inspiring instruction on how to access the power of thought to transform our lives. I am witness to the wisdom released through the Health Realization [*the three principles*] approach. This book is a must read for anyone wishing to create a healthy and fulfilling life.

Cheryl Santacatarina
St. Johnsbury, VT

I've been around this understanding for nearly 10 years and it has been helpful personally and professionally; but since working with Jack, my understanding has deepened significantly. Jack's warmth, understanding, deep-seeing, and unwavering faith in my own innate health and wisdom has helped me to really see the principles of Mind, Consciousness, and Thought creating my moment-to-moment experience. Most importantly, he lives what he teaches. Thanks, Jack!

Vince Flammini
Springfield, IL

You know, the only one who helped my thinking shift from a heap of habits to something that is a lot healthier, less habitual and more in tune with who I am is you, and you are on the other side of the world! You pointed me in a different direction, you stayed pretty consistent in not colluding with my habits and you stayed firm in the truth of wisdom within. Everyone needs this.

Georgina Mavor, Psychologist
Western Australia

Health Realization [*the three principles*] has given me the opportunity to experience relief from trauma due to years of abuse. I have begun to see myself and others in a new way. This new way is now filled with compassion and gratitude for what life has given me the opportunity to experience. Being exposed to Health Realization has caused a shift in the way I see my role in life.

Monica
Plainfield, VT

Health Realization has been an amazing journey! By accessing my own health and wisdom I experienced true inner healing. I was then able to (begin to) move forward with my life in peace and joy, with confidence, and with a strength and knowing that was never before present in my life. There is no better way to teach Health Realization than to live it, and Jack Pransky does just that. Through deep listening and accessing his own health and wisdom, Jack is able to cut to the heart of a matter and assist others in the process of healing and self-discovery through the realization of their own inner health and wisdom. Jack's commitment to this inside-out approach to prevention, and to helping others, is impressive and awe-inspiring!

Shelly
Norwich, VT

Through his gifted way of communicating, Jack helps people tap into their own wisdom, even if you think you don't have any. If what you seek is a better, more joyous way of being, the[se] principles for living ...*will* change your life. Just as Jack Pransky has helped me tap the truth within myself, you too will see how to transform your life. I now have a different realization about myself, my relationships, and my work. Instead of carrying around sadness and hopelessness, I now know that every moment holds the possibility for joy.... if I so choose.

Paula Francis
Montpelier, VT

I am able to hang onto good feelings, calm, a peaceful state of mind knowing what I know about my thinking. Jack has helped me to see the connection between my thinking and my consciousness not just through his words, but how he lives his life.

Kellie Joyner
Montpelier, VT

Jack has a way with words that go beyond my intellectual mind and straight into my heart. This feeling comes through in talking and listening with Jack, and in reading his books. It is a refreshing breath that reconnects me to my core...a universal knowing. Life's questions (the BIG ones) do not phase me anymore-for I know these answers already exist within us all.

Amy Dalsimer, Thatcher Brook Primary School
Waterbury, VT

Somebody Should Have Told Us!

(Simple Truths for Living Well)

The Mind-Spirit Connection

Third Edition

Jack Pransky, Ph.D.

CCB Publishing
British Columbia, Canada

Somebody Should Have Told Us!: Simple Truths for Living Well

Copyright © 2011; 2007; 2005 by Jack Pransky
ISBN-13   978-1-926918-26-6
Third Edition

Library and Archives Canada Cataloguing in Publication
Pransky, Jack, 1946-
Somebody should have told us! : simple truths for living well : the mind-spirit
connection / written by Jack Pransky – 3rd ed.
ISBN 978-1-926918-26-6
Includes bibliographical references.
Also available in electronic format.
1. Self-actualization (Psychology). I. Title.
BF637.S4P73 2011   158.1   C2011-900386-4

Book production and design by Burrell Center, Springfield, MO.
Editing by Pam Parrish, Paul Thomlinson, and Amanda Frankel.
Cover design by Trent Schaible.
Cover artwork by Jonas Gerard www.jonasgerard.com

Publisher: CCB Publishing
             British Columbia, Canada
             www.ccbpublishing.com

This book's third edition is dedicated to the memory
of spiritual philosopher Sydney Banks, 1931-2009,
who initially uncovered this understanding
and who personally blew my mind apart with the truth of it.
Words cannot express the gratitude I feel
for this remarkable yet ordinary man
for bringing this inside-out understanding into the world
and being the source and catalyst for touching
and changing so many lives.
The world is a far better place because of his existence.

This book initially was and still is dedicated to the memory of
Susan A. Smith of Bemidji, Minnesota, 1950-2003,
a good friend, an excellent counselor
who touched many lives,
and a beautiful, wonderful human being
whose own life realized even more beauty
through the understanding found in this book.

Acknowledgements

First, I thank every student, trainee, client and community member who has graced me with the honor of opening themselves to listen to this inside-out understanding of the human experience. I have learned so much from you.

Besides Sydney Banks, whom I acknowledged in the dedication, I also sincerely thank Dr. George Pransky (my second cousin) who initially guided me through this understanding.

Thank you to all other teachers of *the three principles* who are spreading this understanding throughout the world and helping so many lives change for the better. To those with whom I have had the pleasure to work alongside thus far—especially Gabriela Maldonado for also contributing wonderful stories to this book—I am grateful to you.

I thank Nancy Greystone who, while serving as my media consultant for my book, *Parenting from the Heart*, inadvertently inspired me to write this self-help book.

I thank Pam Parrish, my initial editor, for assisting me with my writing. And Judy Pransky, Alison Sharer, Kris Washington, Candy Mayer, Georgina Mavor, Diane McMillen, Stephanie Watson and Amy Dalsimer who provided important feedback. Extra special thanks to Dr. Todd Schaible and Paul Thomlinson for their invaluable assistance with initial publishing.

Certainly not least I thank the beautiful people who contributed writings from their own personal experience of what it was like for them to gain this new understanding and turn around their lives. They are living proof that this approach changes lives, and their contributions add much richness and depth that will inspire others.

…a Sioux friend told me:

The Creator gathered all of creation and said,

"I want to hide something from the humans until they are ready for it. It is the realization that they create their own reality."

The eagle said, "Give it to me, I will take it to the moon."

The Creator said, "No. One day they will go there and find it."

The salmon said, "I will hide it on the bottom of the ocean."

"No. They will go there, too."

The buffalo said, "I will bury it on the great plains."

The Creator said, "They will cut the skin of the earth and find it even there."…

Then Grandmother Mole…who has no physical eyes but sees with spiritual eyes,

said, "Put it inside them" [for that is the last place they will look.]

The Creator said, "It is done."

-Gary Zukav[*]

---

[*] Thank you, Ed Lemon

Foreword

Burrell Behavioral Health [the initial publisher of this book] has a long history with Dr. Jack Pransky. In 1991, Jack and Burrell Foundation collaborated to publish *Prevention: The Critical Need*, a book that has helped many individuals, organizations and communities in their efforts to prevent emotional, behavioral and social problems, and which has been used as a college text in many universities. So it was a natural for us to turn again to Jack as we attempted to expand our endeavors in the arena of producing and publishing resources for life and learning. We were pleased to present *Somebody Should Have Told Us!* as the inaugural publication of Burrell Resources for Learning (BRL)... This is a powerful book that further extends the notion that there is nothing wrong with you that can't be fixed by what is right with you.

I spent a lot of time with *Somebody Should Have Told Us!* I mean, I spent many hours, days, and weeks with this book in the process of trying to be a good editor. I really wanted to give Jack some substantive input that he might use to make the book better...you know, cross-referencing the lessons of the book with ancient wisdom literature, current psychological theory and research, and perhaps an occasional pithy poem or song lyric. But, an interesting thing happened as I lived with the book: I began to realize that the wisdom of the book was infiltrating my thoughts, feelings and conversations... I still had my academic, editorial hat on, but found very often that my energy was being directed into applying the lessons of the book to my own heart and mind, both personally and professionally. It has a way of seeping into your life. It seems to me that this is a sure sign of a great self-help book!

You may find yourself (as I did) at first resisting some of the lessons of *Somebody Should Have Told Us!*, just because the path it lays out to health and contentment seems too easy, too simple. How simple? I asked Jack for an essential summary, and here is what he said: "This book is about how we all have a state of perfect Health and wisdom inside us that can only be covered up by our own thinking, and how our thinking creates the 'reality' we see, out of which we then think, feel and act." Actually, that sounds about right, if you believe the ancient wisdom expressed in Proverbs: "As a man thinketh in his heart, so is he." Or if you believe Shakespeare might have known a thing or two about human nature: "There is nothing either good or bad, but thinking makes it so..."(Hamlet). Maybe it really is just that simple. Yet there is no limit to the depth and power of it. Read this book. Soak it in. Then decide for yourself.

Paul Thomlinson
Burrell Behavioral Health
Springfield, MO
August 2005

Author's Note ~ Preface to the Third Edition

It has now been six years since I first wrote *Somebody Should Have Told Us!*. I could not be more gratified by the number of people who have told me their lives have changed as a result of insights gained from reading this book. The way they see life and therefore live life has changed, and their lives are far better for it. They feel better, they act wiser and better things seem to come to them as a result. I am quite humbled by this.

While this warms my heart it is equally true that in the last six years my own understanding has continued to grow. Ironically, my own life has even changed for the better. I see it all so much more simply, clearly and deeply now than I did when I first wrote this book. This caused a conundrum: Since I knew I had to change to a third publisher I wanted to be sure the book reflected my deeper understanding; yet because the book worked so well as written, judging by the feedback I'd received, I was reluctant to make too many changes. Still, I felt I needed to improve the clarity and accuracy of a few items. So rather than rewrite the book I decided to strike a balance by republishing this book as an only slightly-updated third edition, and in the not-too-distant future write Part II.

As you read this I wish you all the peace of mind, well-being, love, high quality relationships and effectiveness in your lives that you wish for yourselves and deserve.

It is there for the taking.

Jack Pransky
Moretown, VT
January, 2011

Preface to the First Edition

Thirteen years ago, in the midst of what I would call a spiritual search—meaning, I read a lot of spiritual books, listened to a lot of tapes, met with spiritual groups, practiced some meditation—suddenly without warning and outside of anything I was examining, my search screeched to a halt. I didn't mean for it to; I didn't even particularly want it to. It happened automatically and effortlessly. I had found what I was searching for.

How did this happen? I only know through my work to prevent problem behaviors I bumped into a new, largely unknown paradigm that turned everything I knew inside-out. At first I couldn't grasp it, but I knew it was important. I heard something deep within my soul that connected with my own wisdom. Consequently I began to live more in well-being. I experienced less stress. My relationships improved. I gained great appreciation for my new understanding.

To my surprise I then discovered I could help others find for themselves what I had found. They too began to experience more well-being and their problems dropped away. I was onto something that worked more powerfully than anything I had encountered. It became my life's work. It has helped many people gain a sense of mental and spiritual health, balance and peace of mind.

I take no credit for this. All I do is help people connect with their own innate Health and wisdom. Most people, it seems, are not guided by their wisdom.

I never thought I would write a self-help book. It happened serendipitously. While on a publicity push for my book, *Parenting from the Heart,* my publicist required me to take media lessons. My tendency when talking with others was to start slowly until I got revved up enough to make my points with a certain power behind them. When talking with the media I didn't have that luxury; by the time I got revved my few minutes were over. So "sound-bite school," as I called it, seemed like a good idea. It helped me hone my important parenting points and put them up front. To find the points I wanted to make I took a walk in the woods to clear my head and allow them to bubble up from within. Interesting thoughts kept arising, but these points seemed important for everyone to know, not just parents; yet I knew almost no one who wasn't a parent (or about to be) would read a parenting book. The thought then popped in, "You need to write a self-help book."

This surprised me. What could I offer that hadn't already been written? Immediately I knew what would set this apart from nearly all other self-help books on bookstore shelves. Most all self-help books tell people what to *do* to improve their lives. Often people read them, find it difficult to put into practice what the books suggest (because their own habits work against them), and nothing changes. Then they read another self-help book in hopes the next one will help.

Instead, what if people were pointed inside themselves to the source of their own answers? What if they were helped to see the "mechanism" at work behind how they function psychologically and spiritually? What if they were helped to see the principles behind what creates their very experience of life? Pointed in this direction they would have the key to unlock their wisdom to guide them through any difficulty. They could take it with them wherever they go—always—because it is already part of them. They only need to *see* it! Once they saw it they would no longer need any self-help books—including this one. I have seen dramatic changes in people's lives result from helping people see life from the inside-out. My intent is simply to be of service to as many people as I can. A book potentially can reach a far greater number than those with whom I can work personally or in training groups.

I truly believe for people to realize how they can use the spiritual, creative gifts they have been given to their benefit instead of to their detriment is the hope for humankind. When wisdom speaks, humanity benefits.

I am merely a ripple in a pond.

A few notes about this book, and how to get the most from it:

➢ Unlike listening to Dr. Phil, Dr. Laura or Dr. Joy Brown, this book contains no advice. It offers no skills, nor any techniques. Initially to some this may be disconcerting, but advice, skills and techniques all reside in the outside world. This book contains something far more valuable. True change happens only from within, from one's own insight. It is far more comforting to realize there really is nothing to do because *we already have everything we are looking for inside us,* and it is always available to us no matter what difficult life situations we encounter—*if* we know how to access it. I don't want anyone looking to me, when the answers are within them. This book points people in the direction of true *self* help.

➢ The only advice I do offer is how to get the most from this book: It would be wise to approach it with an open mind, to clear the mind, to set aside everything you know (at least temporarily), including comparing this to other things. Comparisons and judgments only block new understanding, and new understanding is the whole idea. If you want to truly incorporate into your life what this book offers I suggest reading it again and again until it sounds like old news. Then you will know this understanding has become part of you, the eyes through which you see. You will know you understand when you see the results for yourself.

➢ This book is written the way it is for a reason. It contains a lot of stories and narrative. First, this is because no words can accurately or adequately describe the spiritual—the way it all truly works within us—and stories help point to what I mean. Second, it is often helpful to see through the eyes of what others have gone through.[*] Third, when we become involved in a story we temporarily forget about ourselves and, paradoxically, have a greater chance of having new insights about ourselves. I know that sounds odd, but it's true. Also, this book contains some repetition. I attempt to say the same things in different ways because it helps

---

[*] Note: I have changed the names of some people in these stories, at their request.

the new take hold. Each chapter is meant to build on those before it.

➤ In this book I use some terms for which others have their own definitions, such as Mind, Consciousness, Thought, wisdom, Health, principle. It would be wise to temporarily set aside your own definitions. I explain what I mean when I use these terms. In many places throughout this book I capitalize some of these words when I am meaning the universal, instead of the personal.

➤ The stories in this book are not meant to be an illustration of how to do counseling based on this inside-out approach; they only represent how I worked with these people at that time, for better or worse. Today I may do it differently. But the results speak for themselves.

The state of mind everyone wants for themselves is there for the taking. My hope is this book will help you find the peace you deserve, the peace many are now finding for themselves.

So sit back and relax, absorb and enjoy. It won't do any good to analyze it or try to figure it out. Wisdom comes from the opposite: the uncluttered grace of a relaxed mind.

Jack Pransky
Cabot, VT
January, 2005

Introduction

I felt an explosion of energy inside me. It was impossible that positive self-esteem has always been there and was just covered by negative thoughts!...I could not believe that for the past ten years I have been reading books on self-help, taking seminars, spending lots of money and time and never found an effective way to address the self-esteem problem. I could not believe that it could be so "easy." Feelings of astonishment, incredibility, shame, anger, guilt, relief ran through my whole body... I felt so relieved and full of hope that I could breathe again, but at the same time I was mad. Why didn't anyone tell me this before?

-- Maribel

Somebody should have told us! How come nobody told us?

How come nobody told us how we truly function as human beings, psychologically and spiritually? How come nobody told us how our experience of life is created—how we create for ourselves joyful or miserable lives, peaceful or stressful lives, beautiful or depressed or angry lives?

Why? They didn't know!

Our parents didn't know. Their parents didn't know. Our teachers didn't know. Our mentors and role models didn't know. It's nobody's fault. If they knew they would have told us.

Most everyone would like to live with more peace of mind, less stress and better relationships. The problem is we've been pointed in the wrong direction.

Most self-help books, personal growth seminars and even most counseling and psychotherapy have not told us that peace of mind, little or no stress and naturally fulfilling relationships are already within us—our natural state—and how we're only getting in our own way. The most helpful direction for us is not what we can *do* but what

1

we need to *see* that allows what is naturally within to flow through us unencumbered

Currently, few people have this perspective. Those who do live happy, healthy, fulfilling, productive lives. However, anyone can gain this simple, yet powerful understanding—because it's part of us already! We just don't realize it—yet.

When we see how something really works and see its usefulness we can use that thing to our advantage. If we don't, we're either at its mercy or we're baffled by it or it's luck if it works out. A remote control that runs the TV, DVD, DVR, Tivo, X-Box and sound system can be very useful, but if we don't understand how it functions it is not much use to us and only confuses or frustrates us. The same is true for our own well-being. When we see what makes our well-being come alive within us, when we see what makes us function as we do and how to use it to our benefit, we gain a handle on life. Instead of being at the mercy of our circumstances, instead of being baffled or frustrated by what life throws at us, we discover how we are in charge.

When I look back upon my life, had I known then what I know now I could have spared myself and others so many difficulties. But it's silly to beat ourselves up for what we didn't see. I was innocent. The only way I could have done it differently is if I saw it differently then. The same is true for all of us. The point isn't to look back; it's to live now, armed with the new.

I am not saying difficulties won't happen to us. That is never the case. It's been said many times that "life is a contact sport." But how we experience these so-called difficulties is up for grabs. *What we make of* those difficulties makes the real difference in our lives.

Most of us walk around oblivious to what makes us function as we do, oblivious to what creates our life experience, oblivious to what makes people change, oblivious to what makes people live in well being and with peace of mind. Oblivion is no longer necessary. It is never too late to live with this new understanding for the rest of our lives.

I realized if we deeply understood three spiritual facts or principles, how these facts work together and how our use of them gives us every experience we can possibly have in life, with this perspective we can move through life with peace of mind, well-being, mental health and psychological freedom. These *three principles* are revealed throughout the book. The question becomes, what do we need to know about these three principles and how they work together to help us most in our lives? To that end it occurred to me that The Three Principles point to ten little (but huge) points about life and relationships that would be extremely helpful for people to understand. I don't expect these ten points to mean much as simple statements. Each takes exploration and reflection. Thus, a full chapter is devoted to each:

I.   Our thinking is our life
II.   Wisdom is always available to guide us, if we know how to access it
III.   If someone's thinking doesn't change, they can't change
IV.   When our mind clears our wisdom appears
V.   We don't have to think our way out of our problems (or to happiness)
VI.   The feeling is what counts, and it's foolproof
VII.   What we see is what we get
VIII.   In low levels of consciousness it is unwise to believe, trust or follow our thinking
IX.   To deeply listen to others instead of to our own thinking gives us a richer experience
X.   We're only as stuck as we think we are

To deeply understand the meaning of these statements is to live in a different world, an inside-out world. You may never see yourself or the world in the same way again.

People have within them something so powerful. It is the power to change, to monumental degrees. People are walking potential to change at any moment. They can change their minds, change their thoughts. People have the power to have truly clear minds, and from that clarity to have insights they never before dreamed, insights so powerful the world never looks the same; their lives never look the same. Our innate Health and its natural intelligence is always hidden within us, just waiting to rise to the surface. All we have to do is allow what we think we know to drop away, or no longer take it seriously, and this wisdom will speak to us. It is so close to us that we have forgotten it is there—like the air we take for granted—yet it holds the key that unlocks the potential in everyone. For everyone there is hope out of the destructiveness, out of the depression, the anger, the fear, the insecurity—out of every conceivable emotion and resulting behavior. To access it all we have to do is allow it to come through by recognizing its power in our lives and trusting it.

Thousands of people have now gained this new understanding and have seen their lives improve, many dramatically.

You could be next.

The only requirement is an open mind.

I. Our Thinking is Our Life

Wait! Before you start. I know many of you live with feelings you'd rather not have. I used to too. We live with worry, with stress, with frustration, with anger, bother, anxiety, sadness, depression, jealousy, guilt, with minds too busy, with addiction, and on and on. None of this is necessary. These feelings do not have to rule us. The secret is to understand where these feelings come from, and I don't mean from past events. I mean understanding how all feelings are created within us. I also know from experience you will be able to see this best if we ease into it gradually. Why? Because the information itself means nothing; only your own insights about it make any difference. The mind has to be prepared to take in the new. Don't worry about not seeing it right away; by the end of the book it will have crept up on you and will make complete sense. Then you can read the book again and see even more the next time. We begin with the story of Lisa...

Lisa had never climbed a mountain. She wanted to but was a heavy smoker and afraid she'd never make it. She feared not having the wind or stamina. Over her 39 years others had asked her to go hiking with them. She refused. She was filled with trepidation, and not only about mountains.

As a baby Lisa was abandoned. At 39 she still had never met her real mother. She was brought up by a stepmother, whom Lisa believed hated her. When she was a child her uncle, whom she loved and trusted, sexually abused her. Through such experiences Lisa picked up habits of thinking that at the time helped her survive but as the years went by proved less and less helpful. For twelve years she needed depression medication to get her through the day. She became involved in a series of misguided relationships, at least one physically abusive. She felt stuck. Many things in her life seemed like mountains.

Lisa attended a Three Principles-based course called Health Realization[*] that I taught at the New England School of Addiction Studies. In the class she heard something that touched her deeply. On her way home she realized she actually saw the colors of the trees for the first time. In awe she stood and cried at the beauty. Sporadically over the next few years she counseled with me and attended a long-term professional Health Realization training. She began to see the only thing keeping her stuck was her own thinking.

Through this training Lisa came to realize that she used her thinking in ways that inhibited her, that kept her in fear and longing for a better life. She realized *the only thing in her way was how she used her power of Thought, and her thoughts could change.* With this realization Lisa's life improved dramatically. For the first time she began to experience well-being. She no longer felt the need for depression medication. Her psychiatrically diagnosed "seasonal affective disorder" no longer had the same grip on her. She volunteered to teach what she'd learned to correctional center inmates and began to affect their lives.

Because Lisa's life had changed so, I asked her to co-teach the next Three Principles course with me at the New England School, held that year in southern New Hampshire. During the mid-week afternoon break, for my 56th birthday, I decided to hike Mount Monadnock. I hadn't hiked it since I was a kid. I asked Lisa if she wanted to join me.

"I want to," she said, "but I don't know if I'll be able to do it."

"Lisa," I said, "this is the most climbed mountain in the world. People in far worse shape than you have climbed it."

With all Lisa's other insights about her life she was stuck on the mountain. Why could other people climb mountains and not her? What made her so different?

With mixed trepidation and excitement she decided to try. "If I can do this," she thought, "it would be a huge accomplishment."

---

[*] "Health Realization" is a term used primarily in the past to describe the understanding shared in this book.

So off we went. Lisa spent the entire first part of the climb, which was more like a gentle walk through some pretty woods, grumbling about how unpleasant it was. She wanted to stop and have a cigarette.

"Is this wise?" I asked.

She agreed it wasn't. "But if I have to stop and have one, I'm going to!"

Before we arrived at the steep part of the climb Lisa wanted to quit. She grumbled some more but managed to push on.

After trudging along a while, both of us sweating, we arrived at the steepest part of the climb—solid granite. Suddenly Lisa saw it as a challenge. Her experience of the hike changed. She pulled herself up steep boulders.

"This is fun!" she laughed.

After climbing steep rock for a while both of us were tired. We came to the first beautiful overlook. Lisa had never seen a view like it. She loved it. She thought we were at the top.

"You mean we're not there?" she asked with a pained expression.

"Not yet. It's up there. See?" I pointed.

Lisa became discouraged. Her experience of the hike changed again.

"I don't know if I'm going any further," she grunted, sat down, pulled out a cigarette and lit up.

"Lisa, look, we can see the top! Do you really want to quit now, when we're almost there?"

Lisa grunted again.

A couple of Puerto Rican women, also attending the New England School, appeared on the trail. They didn't feel like going farther either. We chatted a few minutes until some athletic-looking hikers passed by on their way down. I asked them how far it was to the top. They said, "Oh, probably about ten minutes."

"It'll probably take us twenty minutes then," I joked.

For some reason the Puerto Rican women thought that was the funniest thing. They couldn't stop laughing. Amazingly it jazzed everyone up, and we all got up for the last leg.

Grudgingly Lisa put out her cigarette and stood up. "I can't believe I'm doing this."

Twenty minutes later the four of us stood on the peak. Lisa witnessed her first 360-degree spectacular view. Again she stared in awe. Lisa had climbed her first mountain. She had made it to the top.

Lisa made it because she stopped thinking she couldn't.

Most of us don't realize how our thinking controls us. We are at the mercy of our thinking—*until we see and realize how it works to create our experience of life.*

Thought is the greatest gift, the greatest power we have. It is our creative power—the power to create anything with our own thinking. This is the first spiritual Principle. It is a fact. We can have any thought. We generate it. We create it. We make it up.

The second Principle is the fact that we also have another awesome gift: the power of *Consciousness*. Consciousness allows us to experience life. Without consciousness we would not have any experience because we would have no awareness of whatever is happening out there.

Contrary to the way it appears we can never get a direct experience of the world out there through our consciousness. Our consciousness can only give us an experience of what we *think* is out there, of our own interpretation of what is "out there." Our consciousness can only give us an experience of our thinking. *The only experience we can ever have is of our own thinking.*

This statement can be baffling. To truly understand this changes lives.

I'll state this in a different way.

We take in life through our five senses. That's obvious. What isn't obvious is whatever our five senses pick up must be filtered through our own thinking. We can never get a "pure" or direct experience of the outside world. For example, some people looking out a window will see tree branches gently swaying in the wind. Others won't be aware of trees or branches at all; they might see a truck going by. They are looking out the same window at the same stuff at the same moment but are having a different *experience* of what is out there. They are *seeing* a different "out there."

Some people like the taste of broccoli; others don't. Most people love the smell of roses; some don't. Some people love rap music; others can't stand it. Some people love the feel of velour because it reminds them of velvet; the feel of velour used to drive me up the wall. No matter what the sensory organ, it's all how we think about it. It's *only* how we think about it. Always! *We can only know our own personal thinking of the outside world.* That's it. That's all.

In other words, the mountain is not the problem. The mountain is the outside world. Our own thinking about the mountain is the problem. Lisa's experience of the mountain differed from mine because we had different thinking about it and what it meant to us. That was the *only* difference! During the hike Lisa's experience of the mountain changed numerous times. Sometimes it was drudgery, sometimes impossible, sometimes a challenge and fun. Why? Because along the way her thinking changed about it. The point is Lisa is the one who had to live with whatever experience she happened to think up at the time.

This is what happens in life. This is what our life is all about. This is our life, period. When we truly realize everything we experience— our perceptions, our feelings, our problems, whatever we call "reality" or "the way it is"—is really only a product of our own thinking, everything then changes for us. Our experience of life changes.

The outside world can *never* make us feel anything. Only our own thinking can make us feel things. Sometimes in the heat of battle or in a sport such as basketball or football we may not even notice we've been cut—until we notice we're bleeding, and then we think about it. Only then does it hurt. We're not experiencing the pain until we think about it. Our work isn't what's stressing us out; our own thinking about our work is what's stressing us out. It's not Johnny driving us nuts; our own thinking about Johnny is driving us nuts. It's not our fear of speaking in front of a large audience; it's our own thoughts about speaking in front of an audience. It's not the mountain. Our thinking *is* the mountain. Our thinking is what the mountain is to us.

Our consciousness gives us an experience of whatever our thoughts create, and it makes that creation *look real*. That's the job of consciousness: to make everything we believe look real to us. If someone cuts us off in a car nearly causing an accident and we get angry, it seems we really should be angry. But it is only our thinking. I'm not saying what the driver did wasn't wrong or dangerous. I'm not saying we don't sometimes have too much to do in too little time. I'm not saying Johnny doesn't drive a lot of people nuts. I'm not saying there aren't real people in the audience who judge us. I'm not denying the mountain is real. But what determines our *experience* of the mountain—whether we think we can climb it, whether we think we can make it, whether we think it's too much for us, whether we think it's overwhelming, whether we think it's exciting or exhilarating—is *all* determined by our own thinking. Our thinking creates the mountain—for ourselves. Our experience of the mountain is determined by our own thinking. When our thinking changes, our experience of the mountain changes for us.

> First there is a mountain,
> Then there is no mountain,
> Then there is.
>
> -- Donovan
> "There Is A Mountain"

I had no idea what this song meant until I understood this. Like the mountain, our experience of our entire lives is determined by our own thinking—every aspect of life and every situation we encounter. Of course we will encounter challenging times, challenging people, challenging relationships, challenging circumstances. Yet, how we experience these we *make up* with our own thinking—not on purpose, but that's the result.

Our thinking is everything. Life would be nothing for us if it weren't for our thinking. Without our thinking any experience that happens to us would be neutral. Thought provides the content, whether it is good or bad to us, happy or sad or mad to us. With this incredible power of Thought we get to create anything. *We get to create the life we experience.*

Whether we know it or not we are creating our lives constantly, continually. Whatever we happen to see of life changes with our next thought. Some thoughts seem to be more entrenched than others, but even these can change because they are *only thought*.

Suppose we realize that any experience we're having can and will change with new thought. Wouldn't that mean we don't have to take whatever experience we are having now so seriously? After all, whatever we're experiencing will eventually change. Sometimes her fear of the mountain looked real to Lisa; sometimes it didn't. We may be angry at the driver who cut us off now, but a month from now we probably won't be still carrying that around. So why take it so seriously now? We may be stressed because of too much to do at work, but sometimes we're not stressed with the same amount of work. Sometimes Johnny bothers us less than at other times. What is going on? The only difference is our thinking has changed. We don't need to take our momentary, passing feelings so seriously. Our feelings are fluid as our thinking; they are the river flowing by. Why get caught in it?[*] In other words, our relationship with our thinking can change—whether we take it seriously or not, whether or not we believe in it and trust it and follow it.

Thought continually flows within us. God knows where some of the thoughts come from that pop into our heads. We have no control over most of the thoughts that pop in. We can't always decide what we think—that's not our point of choice. Sometimes completely bizarre thoughts come up. If we get a thought of a pink elephant standing on the telephone wires, we may get a picture of it but we won't take it seriously (unless perhaps we're drunk); we will naturally dismiss it. But if we get a thought, "that person doesn't like me" or "that person is ignoring me," those kinds of thoughts we tend to take seriously, even when we have no idea what that person is really thinking.

Who decides what we take seriously?

Tammy feared needles. Because a medical condition required her to get shots from a doctor, this was not good. She avoided her shots because of her fear of needles; therefore, her health worsened. As we

---

[*] Note: I do not mean that feelings aren't important. They *are!* I will explain their importance in Chapter VI.

were talking by telephone about her fear I said something like, "It may hurt a little when you're stuck by a needle, as it would if you were walking down a hallway and brushed against a pin sticking out of a couch, but whether someone sees it with fear or not, they decide."

I don't know what made this pop into my head at that moment, but I flashed upon a time back in 1965 when I took my then-future, now-ex-wife, Judy, to her first visit to New York City. As we stood in her first subway station and the train screeched in Judy stiffened like a board. She clamped her hands over her ears, clenched her jaw, closed her eyes and stood cringing and rigid, while everyone else in the station went about their business as if nothing unusual happened. I asked her what the matter was and she said, "It's too loud for my ears. I have very sensitive ears. I can't stand it!" Every time a new train pulled in she did the same thing. Yet I remembered, over time, as we kept visiting the city she didn't do that anymore. I told Tammy to hang on the phone a moment—she was thinking, "What in the world is he talking about?"—and I ran down the hallway to Judy's office and poked my head in the door.

"Remember when you used to have this horrible reaction to the noise of subway trains coming into the station and now you don't?" I asked. "What changed?"

Judy reflected a moment and said, "I decided not to think about it anymore."

"Ha!" I ran back to the telephone and told Tammy.

"That is very cool!" said Tammy.

We ended the conversation shortly thereafter.

When I spoke with Tammy again a month later I learned she had completely overcome her fear of needles. She got her shots and reported it was no big deal.

What happened?

For whatever reason Tammy realized her fear of needles was just a thought that looked "real" in the moment but actually was just something she made up in her head. Tammy's thinking about needles changed, just as Judy's thinking about subway noise had changed. As a result their experience of these events changed.

Our thinking is our experience of life. Our thinking is our life.

Now standing on the top of the mountain very proud of herself Lisa could not believe what she had accomplished. She couldn't imagine why she had ever thought it impossible, why she had denied herself this experience all those years. Lisa realized the only thing keeping her from climbing mountains was her own thinking. Now she had different thinking; now she had a different life experience.

Could it be that simple?

Yes!

That's the amazing thing about it. It's so simple we haven't been able to see it because it's too close to us.

Earlier I said Lisa is off all depression medication and her "seasonal affective disorder," which used to debilitate her, now affects her very little. How is this possible? None of the many psychiatrists she'd seen over the years could help her get off medication. But when Lisa's thinking changed—when she truly saw the creation of her own experience through her very own power of Thought—when she truly saw her experience of life coming from within her own self, she changed, and her body chemistry changed with it.

I'm not saying this always happens. I'm not saying people can think their way to a changed body chemistry. I am saying when people have an insight of enough magnitude about the true source of their experience, miracles can happen. If I hadn't seen it with my own eyes again and again I might not even believe it—alcoholics and drug addicts who stop using alcohol and drugs and see themselves as "recovered" as opposed to "recovering"; people with a lifestyle of criminal behavior who stop committing crimes; people so stressed out and driving themselves crazy who now live with peace of mind; relationships that were falling apart where now the couple is happier than ever. If I hadn't seen these with my own eyes…

One way to understand Thought is through dandelions. I realized this while mowing my dandelion-riddled lawn. The thought crossed my mind how curious it is that dandelions are seen so differently by different people. In Vermont dandelions are so plentiful they'll take over a field so the entire field turns bright yellow-gold. Contrasted against the emerald green it is quite beautiful—at least I think so. I love the way dandelions look, except when I try to mow my lawn and the blade isn't sharp enough and leaves dandelion parts behind.

To someone who cares about a manicured lawn the dandelion is a nightmare. To a dandelion winemaker the dandelion is a resource. To the herbologist the dandelion is a blessing. To some it is a flower; to others a weed. Other people don't care about dandelions one way or the other. What makes the difference in people's experience of dandelions? Thought and thought alone.

I'm not saying dandelions don't exist unless we think about them. Of course they exist! Of course they are real. I am saying that dandelions do not exist *for us* in a particular moment *unless* we think about them. I am saying that *how* we think about dandelions determines our experience of them. Then we get to live with whatever we experience.

If we see the beauty of this flower covering a field in gold we feel like sighing. If we see the utility of this plentiful flower we appreciate what it can do for us. If we see it as a weed getting in our way, we curse it. The same dandelion can be a beautiful or a miserable experience. All because of the way we think. The same dandelion!

What determines how we think about it? Why do some people end up in one place about dandelions and others in a completely different place?

Because we have deeper, hidden thoughts or beliefs that determine our thinking (and therefore our experience) of dandelions. People with manicured lawns may have something in the back of their heads saying a manicured lawn is of utmost importance. Whatever the reason, that person may not even realize or notice he is carrying around that belief. But when he sees a dandelion he is looking through those beliefs—through that lens—at the dandelion, and that is what determines his experience of the dandelion. The lawn guy will think the dandelion is in his way because it interferes with the manicured lens he is looking through. But the lens he is looking through, too, is self-created. He made it up! He doesn't realize he is getting a bad experience only because of what he himself has made up.

This is what we do with our kids. This is what we do with our neighbors. This is what we do with our partners. This is what we do with our business associates. We have a set of thoughts about what's important about life—from wherever we picked it up—then we look out at the world through that lens and see a distorted vision of the dandelion, person or situation. The lens, however, is not reality; it's only an illusion we have inadvertently created, again with the power of Thought.

Very often we allow someone to drive us crazy because inadvertently we have created the illusion of what people should be like for us. In other words, *we are creating our own misery by what we have made up*—only we don't realize it.

To realize this, to realize what we do to ourselves can be quite humbling. To realize this usually makes us want to take our thinking a little less seriously.

At least it does for me.

We're sitting in a car stopped in traffic next to a large truck. All we can see out our window is a wall of truck. Suddenly we're rolling backwards! We freak out and go for the brake. Only we're not rolling backwards; we're stopped. The truck is really moving forward, but we have the illusion we're moving. That's the thought. We freak and go for the brake because Consciousness gives us a *real,* sensory experience of our thoughts. We would swear we're moving, until we find out we're not. It's our own thinking creating "our reality."

I walked out of my motel room near Detroit, suitcase in one hand, banjo in the other, and my car was not in the parking lot. "What the...?" Maybe it wasn't where I thought I parked it. I walked around the lot. It wasn't there. Close to where I parked I saw a car a little bluer than mine and a little longer than mine, but it wasn't mine. So I walked around the parking lot again. I still couldn't find it. I walked around a third time and still didn't see it. I couldn't believe it. For some reason I didn't panic. I thought it was interesting. Since I was on a book tour and had to get to a book signing a little later in the day I wondered what I would do. Because I hadn't officially checked out yet I dropped my luggage at the front desk and decided to go back to my room and gather myself. As I walked up the stairs to the second floor I put my hand in my pocket for my car keys. They weren't there!

15

"Oh my God," I gasped, "I wonder if I left them in my car last night, and somebody stole my car!"

Instantly I remembered some very loud people in the room next to me late last night as I tried to sleep, and they had left early in the morning, saying, "Hurry up! Shhh! Quick!!"

"Oh no!" I thought, "Maybe they stole my car!"

I walked into the room and immediately noticed my car keys laying on the bed. So much for that theory! Puzzled, I looked out the window overlooking the parking lot and saw a car with a sticker on the back window just like the one my daughter had stuck on mine. "Whoa, that's interesting," I thought. Even more interesting, the car also had a green license plate and, what a coincidence, it was a Vermont license plate and, oh my God, it had the same number as mine, and oh gee, it's my car! I ran downstairs and, sure enough, my car was right where I had left it. It must have been the car that had looked a little bluer and longer than mine.

There are a few possible explanations: 1) I may have been in a time warp, as on *Star Trek*. 2) Someone could have picked my pocket, took my keys, run to my car, drove to the store and zipped back so quickly he slipped the keys on my bed without my noticing. 3) I could be at the first stage of Alzheimer's. More logically, for some reason my car was not in my consciousness, and as a result it did not exist for me at that moment. My car (the fact that it was there) was not in my thinking. Even though I was thinking about finding my car I was not having thoughts of the presence of my car; therefore, my car did not exist for me. This is a perfect example of Thought and Consciousness in action giving me my experience. Weird but perfect.

Like Lisa with the mountain, Tammy with the needles and me with my car, all demonstrate how our thinking is our only experience of life. Our thinking is our life.

II: Wisdom Is Always Available to Guide Us *If* We Know How to Access It

A word of caution: A few people have told me they felt uncomfortable reading this next story. Interestingly, in a perfect illustration of what the last chapter points to, others felt no discomfort. Still others have had important insights from reading this story. The fact is, for better or worse, this story happened exactly as written. I decided not to whitewash it.

Out of the blue a woman named Diane sent me an e-mail telling me how much she appreciated my books. She wrote that Health Realization helped her so much her life was "99.9% better." Only one little thing kept her from total 100% health.

I e-mailed back, "What's that?"

She wrote back saying she'd been having an affair for five years, and that was the one thing keeping her in a state that wasn't perfect health.

"It sounds like you're in pain," I responded.

She wrote back. "Oh my God, I can't believe it! I didn't realize I was in pain, but I am. What you said just turned me around about this, and I know now that I need to end this relationship. I'm ending it right away."

A couple of days later I received another e-mail from her: "I ended it. Everything is fine."

A few days later she wrote back again: "At first the man I was having the affair with was fine, but then he wrote me this long, heart-rending letter, and now I'm really troubled."

It so happened I had an opportunity, on my book tour, to be in the Midwest city where she lived. I asked her if while I was there she would be interested in a counseling session. She said yes.

When I got to town I called her and we arranged a place to meet. It was a beautiful day so she suggested a nice park, which sounded fine to me. When I arrived at our rendezvous spot she had changed her mind and said we should go to a different park, not as pretty but closer. Didn't matter to me.

We parked ourselves at a picnic table. Immediately Diane began talking a mile a minute, telling me she ended that affair but now found herself embroiled in another.

Whoa! I had to shake my head. This was almost too much to comprehend.

Diane was in her mid-40s. She volunteered that she had been sexually abused by her father for many, many years and was pretty much a mess because of it. She told me she recently spent a lot of time working out at a gym and had lost twenty pounds. She dressed provocatively to show it. It wasn't hard to tell she wanted men to notice her. Apparently it was working because in the gym this new guy became attracted to her. They went out together, then started having sex.

Listening deeply to her, something nagged at me. I couldn't put my finger on it. I didn't know Diane, but she seemed extremely uncomfortable. Something was up that she wasn't telling me. I kept listening. She told me how this new guy was giving her advice about how she should be with her husband.

"Diane, let me get this straight," I said. "The guy you're having an affair with is giving you marital advice?"

She said, "Yes, because I haven't known what to do with my husband. Our sexual relationship isn't good at all. I think my husband is gay. I love him as a friend but there's no real intimacy in our relationship."

"Whoa, Diane, slow down." It was hard to get a word in edgewise. "Let's back up a moment and take one thing at a time. First, do you really think this guy is in a position to give you advice about your marriage? He's having an affair with you! Do you really think those two things mix?"

Diane began looking very sheepish. "I wasn't going to tell you this," she said, "but he's here."

"What?"

"He's sitting in a car over there watching us, to make sure that nothing goes wrong."

"You're kidding, right?"

"No. He is."

"Diane, come on! Do you really think we can get anything accomplished with you being distracted about the fact that this guy is here?"

"No."

"You need to ask him to leave."

"I can't do that."

"Why not?"

"Because I just can't."

I'm thinking, "If you don't, kiddo, this session is over." I mean, it was freaky enough to think we were being spied on. Besides, I didn't know this guy, and she had only known him for two weeks. For all I knew he could be dangerous. But I didn't want to alarm her with that thought; mostly I wanted her to come to her own conclusion.

"Look," I said, "What is your wisdom telling you to do about this?"

"I can't tell him. That's not the kind of person I am."

"That's not what I asked, and yes you can. You know what's right. He's over there spying on you. I repeat, what is your wisdom telling you to do about this?"

Diane reflected a moment. "I guess I have to tell him to leave," she sighed.

"You're right, and if he doesn't leave when you ask him, that will tell you a lot about him, won't it?"

"Yes."

I prepared her a little for what she might say if he didn't leave, and she got up and walked over to tell him.

I kept my eyes glued to the table in front of me, hoping the guy wouldn't do something we'd all regret. Apparently I hadn't listened to my own wisdom when I agreed to meet this strange woman in a park.

After a few minutes Diane came back and said, "I told him to go." She felt good she followed her wisdom and was strong enough to do it.

"Great," I said. "I knew you could do it."

"But he said something really weird at the end there."

"What's that?"

"He said, 'You know you're going to be thinking about me, whether I leave or not.'"

I sat up straight. "Diane, what do you think he's trying to tell you? Doesn't that sound a little off to you?"

"Yeah." She peered over to where he'd been. "You know what? I think he just moved to a different part of the park. I don't think he left altogether because he's got to drive by here to get out, and I didn't see him drive by." She couldn't see him though.

"Do you think that's a problem? Are you going to be able to focus?"

"I am. I know him. He's not going to cause a problem."

"Okay, but as I said, if he hasn't left after you asked him to leave that tells you something about him, right?"

"I know."

We walked into the middle of an open field away from any cars and where we could see anyone approaching. Diane again started to speedily ramble on about what she'd learned from Richard Carlson's book, *You Can Be Happy No Matter What*, and how it had helped her.

I said, "You know what? I don't really care what you know. I'm glad the book brought you out of your depression, but what matters now is what more you can know to get yourself living more in well-being. Besides, happiness is overrated. What you really want is peace of mind."

Diane quieted for the first time. She nodded and said wistfully, "Yes, that's what I want."

Softly I said, "It's there for you, you know?"

"What do you mean?"

"Peace of mind is built into us. The only thing that can get in its way is our own thinking. We don't have to think anything to be in peace of mind. In fact, when we're not thinking anything we automatically have peace of mind."

I talked about how we have two voices inside us: our voice of wisdom that speaks very softly, and our habitual thinking—our typical, everyday habits of thinking—that speaks loudly. We get to choose which voice we want to listen to. It's very tempting to listen to the loud voice.

"Yes, I've got to try to drop those thoughts. I've got to try and reach a tranquil state."

"It's not really that. It's knowing which voice is speaking to us at any time, and truly knowing which one is good for us to listen to and which isn't. We get to decide for ourselves which to give power to. That's all there is to it. That voice of habit will keep talking to us. It will keep trying to get us to pay attention, but if we know listening to it is not going to serve us well, we're in the position to decide whether to listen to it or not."

That seemed to calm Diane. She said, "Thank you so much! I don't want to take up any more of your time. I feel so much better."

"Wait," I said. "There's one more thing we ought to deal with. There's your peace of mind in general, but there's also your immediate situation. The fact that your situation remains unresolved in your mind means you're going to be thinking about it, and that's going to get in the way of your peace of mind. Wouldn't you want to start with a clean slate?"

She hadn't told her husband about either of these affairs.

I asked her, "Do you love your husband?"

She gave me an immediate "Yes." She had two kids. She said the older one was deaf and very sweet, thirteen years old; the younger one, seven years old, was very angry. Apparently a lot of bickering occurred in their household.

"I may have to leave this relationship," Diane mused, sadly.

"Look, if you love him, there's a solid foundation there. But what does your wisdom tell you about where your relationship can go with your husband if you're involved in these affairs and there's always something hovering over you that you're hiding from him?"

She sighed, "I really need to get out of this affair totally."

"See, this is your wisdom speaking to you now. Can you hear the difference in the voices?"

"Yes. I know I've got to end it with this guy immediately."

"And then there's the fact of your husband not knowing, and you keeping this secret and hiding it."

"I know. I've got to tell him."

We talked about how he might react.

I said, "Then there's a third thing." Diane and her husband supposedly had a solid friendship relationship, but she'd said she thought he might be gay. Was he really? What if he didn't care for her sexually? Sex was obviously extremely important to Diane.

"If he is gay," I asked, "how do you think he would react if you both got your sexual gratification elsewhere?"

"No way! He's a strict Lutheran. He would never be able to handle that."

"Well, what about him? What does he do?"

"He gets his gratification by going onto the Internet and looking at naked men, and he got his penis pierced and all this kind of stuff."

"So there's something he feels a need for that is outside of your relationship too; in fact, outside of himself."

"Yeah."

"And what about you?"

"Well, I've got all these sex toys."

I'm thinking, "Whoa, this is a world I know nothing about. In fact, I don't want to know anything about it." So I said, "Look, if there's a solid foundation in your relationship and everything is honest and on the table, doesn't your wisdom say that you could come to a meeting of the minds about this?"

"Yes. But how?"

"Your wisdom will tell you if you get quiet. One possibility is you could go out of your way to really listen to him deeply so you can see his world the way he sees it and be fascinated by what would make him want to do those things. Then he could do the same with you. When the two of you are able to see each other's worlds, you then have a chance of coming to a meeting of the minds about what you could do together to make your relationship satisfying for each other."

"Yes, that is really, really important for us."

"Which voice is speaking to you about this now?"

"This is definitely my wisdom."

"Then you know what wisdom sounds like. You know what to do. It's always there to guide you. You can never go wrong if you listen to it."

Diane got teary-eyed and thanked me profusely. Our session ended. She went off to see whether that guy was still in the park, and I left.

Later I learned he hadn't left the park. That sealed it. Diane put an end to that relationship. She told her husband about the first affair at least, and they began a healing process.

When it comes to wisdom we are always at a fork in the road. We can listen to it or not.

Fortunately, we are not left to the devices of our own thinking. If the power of Thought is a creative gift we can use in any way we want, and if the power of Consciousness is a gift that makes whatever we're thinking look real to us and gives us the experience of whatever we're thinking, where do these phenomenal powers or gifts come from?

They come from something we could call "Universal Mind." Mind is the third (actually, the first) of *three Principles**—Mind, Consciousness and Thought—that work together to create our life experience. I'm not talking about our own little minds here. I'm talking about something way bigger than ourselves that flows through us. I'm talking about the force or energy that keeps us alive. What it is is a mystery, but it is the energy behind all life that seems to have an intelligence attached. I'm talking about something of which we are one little part: One huge Intelligence or Mind; the Energy of All Things. If you don't like the term "Mind," call it whatever you want. It doesn't matter.

---

* By "Principle," I mean the root of the word: "a fundamental law or truth" that exists as a fact whether people know about it or not. For example, by this definition three principles work together to create a musical note from a stringed instrument: the tightness of the string, the thickness of the string and the length of the string. Depending on how we use those principles, we get different notes. In a similar way, Mind, Consciousness and Thought are the principles at work in the psychological-spiritual world to create our experience. How we use them gives us different experiences.

What matters is that we are a little tiny piece of this formless, universal intelligent energy that flows through us continually and never stops. It can't stop, for it is the life-force itself. Without it we wouldn't exist. That is a fact! What matters is when we're in touch with that tiny little piece of infinite Intelligence, we can hear wisdom speaking to us.

Wisdom, then, as I mean it, doesn't really come from us, per se; it comes through us. Wisdom is something that never goes away. It is always there, *able to be accessed at any moment*. The only way wisdom could disappear is if Mind disappeared, and that is impossible because life itself would cease to exist. Even if we wanted to get away from our wisdom, we couldn't.

This raises a question: If people have all this wisdom, why do most people walk around looking like they don't have it?

Our thinking obscures our wisdom, indeed, it is the only thing that can. Our thinking obscures our wisdom the way a veil covers a beautiful sculpture. Even though we can't see the sculpture, it is there. Our thinking is the veil. When the veil is pulled off the sculpture it is there for everyone to see because it never went anywhere in the first place. We can have faith in that. We could have the same kind of faith in our wisdom and innate Health.

Because Diane's thinking was so scrambled she could not see her wisdom. Once her mind calmed down her wisdom appeared. It was there all along. She only couldn't hear it because of the noise in her head.

The two voices—wisdom and our typical thinking—are always speaking to us. We can notice the difference. If we listen closely we would notice our habits of thinking sound like old news. Many times before we've had these types of thoughts. That voice tends to grab us. It's enticing. On the other hand our wisdom has an "Oh yeah, I see it!" or an "ah-ha" or "ah, yes," feeling attached, a solid knowing deep within ourselves. Everyone has experienced both. The decision about which voice to listen to can be the difference between living a life of well-being or a life of problems and difficulties. All we have to know is how to access this wisdom [see Chapter IV].

Postscript: The next Spring and then the following New Year's I received e-mails from Diane, which I combined here:

Guess what Jack?! I finally got it. I am now living for today only. I realized " I AM "...I am NOW. God is and always has been NOW... No worrying about yesterday or what will happen to me tomorrow or "me" in general. I noticed colors are brighter too. The bad habit of daydreaming is almost gone. When I start thinking about something that isn't...relevant to what is important NOW, then it isn't worth thinking about. It makes my mind more clear to think, and it seems to flow better. Also, I stopped looking at men to see if they're looking at me... It's cool. Life is good NOW. And if it isn't, the next moment will be... I am free!!!... Free from everyone finally and for good... I tell it like it is fully and leave out nothing. Truth all the way...I am free of all guilt, and I am happy with me (because being a "totally" a good girl is what makes me feel good, strong and real). I have no burdens on me anymore...I am entering a weight lifting contest (my first) in March. It's a new beginning... So, now nothing bothers me anymore. It's a miracle. A wonderful gift I have for the New Year... I am so comfortable in my skin it's corny. I think I look the best I've ever looked... It shows on the outside how wonderfully free I feel on the inside...and I keep it good and wholesome... Jack ,it's nice to feel good about yourself, huh?

25

Maribel's Story

What follows is the first of a series of personal stories, written by individuals in their own words, after they experienced insightful changes in their lives as a result of being exposed to the understanding of The Three Principles. These stories are interspersed between many of the chapters. Each is not meant necessarily to reflect the point of the previous chapter; rather, all the stories are meant to demonstrate what can happen when people have deep personal insights about the points made throughout this book.

Maribel is a construction worker who attended a workshop Gabriela Maldonado and I conducted in Puerto Rico. In the middle of the workshop something happened to her. Later she wrote this:

At the Living in Well-Being workshop Jack drew a circle. On the inside of the circle, when he asked us to think of a time in our lives when we were in well-being, he wrote all the positive feelings we felt. Then he drew another circle around the other one, but in this one he wrote our negative thoughts. He explained that the circle inside was full of the positive feelings that are innate within us, and the negative emotions are created by our thoughts during our lives. He said that the positive feelings have always been there, and they are still there. We do not have to create them.

Suddenly he wrote the word "self esteem" on the inside circle. I felt an explosion of energy inside me. It was impossible that positive self-esteem has always been there and was just covered by negative thoughts! And if I am the one who creates the negative thoughts, it means I can also eliminate them. So what I have to do is to eliminate the negative thoughts and the positive ones will appear, which creates a healthy self-esteem.

I could not believe that for the past ten years I have been reading books on self-help, taking seminars, spending lots of money and time and never found an effective way to address the self-esteem problem. I could not believe that it could be so "easy". Feelings of astonishment, incredibility, shame, anger, guilt, relief ran through my whole body.

I was so worried because I thought I had the responsibility to help my 13 years old son with his low self-esteem problems. That feeling was asphyxiating me; I was worried 24/7 because it was very difficult for me to reason with him. Creating a positive self-esteem for him was like constructing a skyscraper, a humongous task, and I needed to build it fast because things were getting rough. He even jumped from a second floor to feel accepted by his peers.

Jack told me that his positive self esteem has always been there too, that there was no need to build anything. I just needed to help him realize where his negative thoughts were coming from—himself—and liberate the positive ones. I felt so relieved and full of hope that I could breathe again, but at the same time I was mad. Why didn't anyone tell me this before? Why did my son have to suffer so much? I though it was an injustice; I did not know how could I be so blind.

I could not stand the feelings, so after Jack called for a break at the workshop I went out of the building and took a walk through a backyard. I walked trying to calm and pardon myself. For the first time I could understand what deep listening* was and what a bad listener I was. The deep listening experience made me understand why my kids always complained that I never listened to them. Now I know they were right. I thought of how many painful situations I could have avoided if I only would have listened to my daughter. She is now 17 years but her wisdom surpasses her age. Now I know she has been giving me good advice, talking to me since she was a year and a half, but since adults are told that they are wiser than kids, I underestimate her. I lost 15 years of intrinsic wisdom of another human being.

Not only that, Jack also taught me that my tormented relationship with my daughter was not really because of her strong temper, nor because she is an Aries and I am a Libra,

---

* Note: "Deep listening" is described in Chapter IX.

nor because she is active and I am calmed, but because since she was two weeks old I established in my mind that she would be a strong, hard-headed, impatient girl. Ever since, I have been trying to prove my theory right. So I could not understand when people told me how joyful, caring and well behaved she was. I got to think that she had a dual personality or had something against me. Now I know it was a presumption established in my mind.

After the workshop I talked to my daughter and told her what I learned, gave her a big hug and thanked her for being so patient with me. She was happy and told me she never understood why I could not understand how people liked to be with her when I said she was too bad tempered. Now I am full of hope for a new beginning.

After the seminar I went to the beach to think and organize all my new knowledge. I wanted to see how these experiences would change my life and those around me. I promised myself I would apply all what I learned a day at a time in order to be able to surpass certain circumstances.

It is like a baptism, a cleaning for my beautiful soul, a cleaning of all the negative thoughts I had inside. I started a new life. I was a new person. When I see pictures of when I was younger, I see the same body, but still a different person. I even feel pity for the woman I see, because I know how much she is suffering, missing and wasting. I know it is impossible to go back. It is a path that I already walked; deep inside I do not want to go back. I want to be happy, I am entitled to it, I am going to "fight" for it, and I will follow the path of my soul because I came to follow the light, the energy source of love.

III. If Someone's Thinking Doesn't Change, They Can't Change

For some reason humans seem to want to change other humans, especially those they care about most. We can try until we're blue in the face to change others, but we can't.

We say to our kids a million times, "pick this up and put it away," and the next time we come around the corner it is still not picked up and put away. Sure, we could force them or punish them or provide consequences, but that is not the point. We wanted to change their behavior, we told them what we wanted, they heard us, and nothing changed. This is puzzling.

It is only puzzling because we're not inside their heads. If we were inside their heads we would see that despite our saying "pick this up, put that away," nothing about their thinking has changed. So long as they are still thinking the same they are going to leave their stuff around. If they're still thinking the same way, they have no choice but to do the same thing. We can only do what our own thinking tells us.[*]

A sexual predator gets picked up, gets thrown in jail, goes through treatment and comes back home. Do we expect his behavior to change? I guarantee his behavior will not change *unless* his thinking has changed. I guarantee he will not commit any other harmful acts *if* his thinking is aligned with his wisdom. If that offender can be helped to see how he uses his own power of Thought to create the way he sees himself, to create what he sees of his "victim," to create what he sees of the situation, to create what he sees of life—out of which he then thinks, feels and acts—then he has a chance to change. Without this understanding what he sees is *real* to him and he has no choice but to

---

[*] Even if someone is pointing a gun at us, ultimately we still decide with our own thinking whether to do what he says or say, "I'd rather die."

29

act on (or fight against) the reality he sees. If we are able to help him see that what he feels compelled to act upon is *not reality* but is inadvertently made up with his own thinking, we have a shot at helping his behavior to change because he will see with new eyes. If not, we leave change to chance. *A change of thought is the only thing that can ever work to change behavior.*

This is true for all of us.

If we have an eating problem we may be worried about our weight or the way we look. If our thinking does not change about our relationship to food, our relationship to our weight, our relationship to how we look, we can try to diet for the rest of our lives but will revert back to what our thinking is telling us.

Suppose we'd like to change the way our partner treats us in a relationship. Unless our partner's thinking changes, our partner will never change. Even if we have only a slight annoyance with something our partner does, can we really expect our partner's behavior to change if his/her thinking doesn't change?

In my family I grew up having to do the dishes but not having to clean the kitchen counters. When I finished washing the dishes my job was done, and I would go about my business. I carried this thinking into my marriage. I had no problem doing dishes because it's part of my thinking. Cleaning counters was not. No matter how much my ex-wife, Judy would have liked me to clean the counters, unless something changed about my thinking I wouldn't be cleaning counters. When I finished the dishes she either had to remind me to clean the counters or they wouldn't get done—unless she cleaned them, which she had to do regularly. I even wanted to do the counters—for her—but I never thought about it. She thought I was incompetent when it came to cleaning the kitchen.

Gradually I started to see the folly of my ways. Counters began to seep into my consciousness (my thinking). Sometimes I found myself actually noticing the counters after doing dishes. Not always but sometimes. Slowly my thinking started to change about the importance of clean counters. I'm not even sure how it happened.

Judy grew up in a family where she was responsible for the cooking and cleaning for her parents' entire family of ten kids. Because she was the oldest girl in the family all responsibility seemed to fall upon her. She considered herself finished in the kitchen when everything was scoured and shining beautifully and she took the strainer out of the sink drain and laid it on its side. She carried this thinking into our marriage.

It completely baffles me why anyone would want to take the strainer out of the drain, because when people later rinse off a dish and the strainer is not in the drain, I end up having to pick the garbage out of the drain before I can put the strainer in so I can wash the dishes. This makes no sense to me. But as many times as I said this to Judy it didn't sink in—literally—because it was still part of her thinking that when she was finished with the kitchen and everything was clean, the proof was the strainer laying on its side in the sink.

This used to really bother me. Once I came to understand Thought I never expected the strainer to be in the drain—unless Judy happened to have a new realization. When I understood this it no longer bothered me. I became fascinated that the drain stopper was never where I thought it should be and I always had to go through the process of picking garbage out of the drain opening. Now I thought it was funny.

It had driven Judy nuts that I didn't clean the counters to her satisfaction. It had driven me nuts that I always had to pick garbage out of the drain. Our thinking had formed our respective views; our ways of seeing it had become ingrained in our thinking.

Can it ever change? Of course! But perhaps not so easily because of our ingrained habits. Obviously, these are not the most important issues in the world—it seems silly to even bring it up—but sometimes little irritants pile up and get to people and before anyone realizes what's happening there's a big problem in the relationship.

When Judy and I both started to see what was going on, unless she was in a bad mood Judy cheerfully came around behind me when I forgot and cleaned the counters. Unless I was in a bad mood I cheerfully knew I would be picking out the garbage from the drain opening before I began the dishes. The reason we became cheerful about it was because we saw it as no big deal, and we didn't take it personally. After all, how big a deal is it if either one of us spent a few extra seconds in my case, or a few extra minutes in her case, doing things the way we would each like them done?

Probably we both could have changed had we sat down and had a heart-to-heart talk about the importance of counters and drains. If I really grasped "counters" the way Judy grasped counters my thinking and therefore my behavior would change about them and the issue would have disappeared. If Judy grasped "strainers" the way I grasp strainers her thinking would have changed and the issue would have disappeared. But in this case because we no longer saw these issues as a big deal, having a heart-to-heart talk about it just didn't seem necessary. With larger issues it might have. It's interesting to me how those little irritants used to bother us and they stopped. Why? Because I knew, no matter what the issue, if my partner's thinking didn't change my partner's behavior wouldn't change, and vice-versa.[*]

Is it possible to change someone's thinking?

It really isn't. People's thinking changes *only* when they have an *insight* of enough magnitude, and insight is the one thing we cannot make happen in another person. We can't even make an insight happen in ourselves.

Insights are very mysterious; they emerge on their own in their own time, like an air bubble rising to the surface in water. When the bubble reaches the surface it pops. That's our insight. We can't change others because we can't make them have insights, but we may be able to put them in a position to increase their chance of having insights. [More in Chapter IV.]

Most of us like our own thinking. We all tend to think our way is the right way. We don't want to change. But the other person feels the same way. This is called "separate realities." Neither of us wants to change. However, if it would create a great relationship, wouldn't we want to be open to seeing new?

---

[*] Our eventual divorce, years later, had nothing to do with issues like this. It had to do with listening to wisdom.

Bruce is a marketing specialist. He had been a marketing specialist for two or three different fast food companies. He was so good at his job that profits increased in each of the companies at which he worked. Bruce played a key role in building a small, family-owned California company into a franchise that expanded into many other markets. When the company grew large enough the owners decided to issue stock options. They then became concerned about what their stockholders would think.

After profits increased for many quarters, one quarter they suddenly leveled off. Bruce knew why: Other people in the company had made some bad decisions. He tried to talk to his bosses. The largest stockholders, however, believed the leveling of profits was the fault of the marketing department. Bruce was in charge of marketing. Out of nowhere Bruce was fired. His bosses, with whom he'd had a great relationship, went along with the stockholders. It was business, nothing personal.

Bruce was devastated. He felt the company screwed him. He felt it was a reflection on him. He wanted to be appreciated for his work. Instead he was out on the streets in the cutthroat world of big business. Torn apart, he began to lose confidence. Bruce became furious with his former bosses and the entire company. He became terribly stressed and it affected his usually fun-loving demeanor.

Because I liked Bruce a lot, when I heard this I sent him George Pransky's old tape on "forgiveness."* By this time Bruce had secured a job with another fast food company and had to move his entire family half-way across the country. His family was not pleased, but they had little choice.

One day Bruce told me, "You know, listening to those tapes really didn't do anything for me about forgiving this other company, but I'm suddenly looking at my work with completely different eyes."

I had no reason to doubt Bruce, but I also knew while he is a great guy he is very competitive, and he's especially hard-driven about his job. When he believes something is right he goes after it with a

---

* George Pransky is my cousin and mentor in originally helping me grasp this inside-out understanding. This tape is among many that may or may not still be available from Pransky & Associates: (360) 466-5200.

vengeance until he gets his way. He has great confidence in his marketing abilities and knows his ideas work better than most other people's. So despite what Bruce told me I wasn't convinced his thinking had changed—until I went to visit him. He described how the president of his new company was making decisions based on what seemed to be his own personal interests, which didn't seem to be in the best interests of company reputation or profitability. This was a hands-on president who had the final say on everything. The company's employees were up in arms, believing some of his decisions would send the already-struggling company down the tubes.

Yet something strange had happened. In the midst of this conflict I noticed Bruce was very peaceful. People in his company were coming to him tearing their hair out, asking him why he wasn't upset.

Bruce said simply, "Look, he's made up his mind. There's nothing we can do about it. We've tried to tell him otherwise and for whatever reasons he's not listening. It may mean this company ends up going down, but our job is to produce the best product we can under the circumstances, give him what he wants, and that's the way it goes. We have no control over anything else."

I couldn't believe my ears. Bruce was peaceful! He knew the president was making a mistake. Bruce would offer his opinion if asked, he would strongly present his case, but once the president actually made his decision, if he didn't like it he could leave or learn to live with it. Despite how bad Bruce thought the decision, he wasn't going to let it bring him down. Before, Bruce would have practically beaten down the president's door to get him to see the light. He also knew others had been fired for doing the same.

Bruce said to me, "I can't even believe I'm saying this: Why bother to get upset about things you have no control over? It doesn't make any sense."

Bruce's entire demeanor changed about work. He no longer took personal responsibility for what happened in the company, even if it went under. He would simply do the best job he could and let the chips fall where they may. After all, once the president made up his mind, what good would it do to continue to argue and get fired? The decision would still be made. Bruce no longer drove himself crazy about work while at home. The difference in him astonished me. He was pretty astonished himself.

Anyone's thinking can change with new insight, no matter how entrenched they seem.

We can be sure of only one thing: When our thinking changes, our experience changes of whatever is going on. Bruce's thinking changed about his job. Before his change he never would have believed he could be a different person at work. Once his thinking changed his experience at work, his feelings naturally changed. Bruce changed because his outlook changed, and outlook is thought.

It is the only way people can change.

It is my observation that most people who have written about consciousness over the years have missed the link between Thought and Consciousness. The two are, essentially, one and the same. What would cause our consciousness to rise? If we don't understand its link to Thought, this is a mystery—all we can do is resort to techniques such as meditation or Yoga or other spiritual practices to try to raise our consciousness. But if we look closely we can see *our consciousness rises or falls as the quality of our thinking rises and falls.*

Consider seatbelts. When seatbelts first appeared I did not have their use in my consciousness. I had heard stories of people wearing seatbelts who had gotten into bad accidents and couldn't escape because they couldn't free themselves. So in my mind I was not going to wear a seatbelt.

I don't know what happened but over the years I began to realize that situations where people had rolled over in their car and were sitting in a river upside-down and couldn't get out of their seatbelts were rare indeed, compared with the lives and injuries saved by wearing seatbelts. I wasn't even aware my thinking about seatbelts had changed, but it did. With it my consciousness of seatbelts changed. Now if I get into a car and don't put on my seatbelt I feel naked, as if something is missing. Seatbelts are now embedded in my consciousness, embedded in my thinking, and I don't have to go out of my way to think about them. Putting on my seatbelt is automatic, but it is still Thought. A thought I don't know I'm having is telling me, "Put on your seatbelt." That thought goes by so fast and it's so much a part of me now that I never have to consciously think about it. When my thinking about seatbelts changed, my consciousness and my experience about seatbelts changed, therefore I changed about seatbelts.

Alcoholics have alcohol on their minds; therefore alcohol is in their consciousness. Recovering alcoholics also have alcohol on their minds—only different thinking is attached so they have different, higher consciousness about alcohol. They still may think about alcohol a lot, but they may also think, "If I go to A.A. meetings every week [or every day] and check in with my sponsor when times are rough, I'll be okay." Therefore, so long as they go to meetings and check in with their sponsor everything is okay. Other people don't have alcohol or drugs on their minds at all; they don't even think about alcohol or drugs. I am one of those people. If someone hands me a beer I may drink it but I never go out of my way to seek it. People like this are at peace with alcohol and therefore have an even higher consciousness about it because of different thinking. There are other things I have a lower consciousness about.

Everything we see in this world works the same. Our levels of consciousness change with our thinking, as we see the world through that different thought-lens.

In any moment how we see any situation can change. Remember, we have essentially made up what we see; it's an illusion of our own creation. When we truly realize *we are making it up*, we automatically change because the way we see it all suddenly changes and our level of consciousness rises.

I can't force this to happen in anyone, but I might be able to help someone see what I see about how experience is created—if that person is open enough to hear it. This allows greater opportunity for people to change on their own. Only if people's thinking shifts on its own from the inside can they really change. This goes for us, too. If our thinking changes we will change, and if it doesn't we won't.

36

IV. When the Mind Clears, Wisdom Appears

While writing my doctoral dissertation the thought suddenly occurred to me, "Man, I am not at peace."

Because of what I supposedly knew this was quite puzzling to me. True, I had far too much to do in far too little time. I had many other things going on in my life while scrambling to complete my dissertation. I had a deadline.

Then I remembered I had set my own deadline. I made that up! This amused me. I was driving myself crazy with a deadline I had set for myself.

Still I wondered why I wasn't able to write this dissertation with peace of mind. I knew enough to get curious. I didn't try to analyze it or figure it out; I knew that would only clutter my mind more. So I quieted my mind.

Out of that quiet, out of that reflection, into my head popped an answer: "I'm not at peace because I have a head full of evaluation."

The thought surprised me. I had never realized that before.

What did my "head full of evaluation" look like? It took the form of "Am I doing enough?" and "Am I doing well enough?" Such thoughts were on my mind continuously.

I knew instantly where I picked up those thoughts. They were drilled into my head when I was a kid. I had to be doing something productive, and I had to do it well. At least that's what I came to think from whatever I heard my parents say. They never even used those words! Regardless, it was all in innocence. When parents lay things on their children it is usually with the best of intentions. After all, it makes perfect sense; most parents would love their kids to be productive, do well and take pride in what they do. But somehow it got into my consciousness as "You've got to do enough" and "You've got to do it well enough." The problem was not at all whatever my parents said; the problem was how I innocently took it in. Without realizing it these thoughts were cluttering my mind and so long as they cluttered it I could not be at peace. The problem was not that such thoughts are bad ideas—they aren't; the problem was they were in my head without my knowing it, interfering with my peace of mind. They were interfering with my productivity because my energy was being siphoned off by these distracting thoughts and therefore not fully devoted to the task at hand.

Once I saw this I couldn't believe how often those thoughts appeared in my head. They dive-bombed me; I almost felt I had to duck. But I knew it was just a habit of thinking I'd picked up. They were so ingrained I knew I couldn't stop them from entering my mind. Instead I allowed them to flow through me unencumbered. I simply saw them for what they were—just habits of thinking I had innocently picked up that didn't have to rule me. So in they came, and out they went—like breathing. They no longer affected me.

Because I saw them for what they were this thinking gradually began to diminish. It still rears its head from time to time, especially when I'm in a low mood, but now when they appear I simply remember those thoughts are nothing but an old habit that doesn't mean anything.

What was I left with when those thoughts stopped gripping me? Peace of mind.

I still had the same amount of work to do in the same limited time. But now I worked with peace. The work didn't change, the time frame didn't change; the only thing that changed was my thinking. Knowing this quieted my mind, which allowed wisdom to rise to the surface. Now I was more productive. Now I could devote my energy directly to the task at hand and not have it siphoned off in directions that did not serve me well.

Our wisdom is infinite intelligence always speaking to us. There is one catch: *We can only hear it with a clear mind.*

In every workshop I conduct I nearly always ask people, "Where are you or what are you doing when you get your best ideas?"

Invariably people say things such as, "When I'm in the shower," "When I'm driving," "Just before going to sleep," "As I'm waking up," "When I'm washing dishes," "When I'm gardening," "When I'm running," "When meditating," "When taking a walk."

The specifics don't matter. What is the common denominator? People's minds have calmed down. When the mind calms and quiets or clears we can hear our wisdom speak. It is the *only* time we can. This is the simplicity.

George Pransky uses a metaphor I find myself using a lot: Our wisdom is always playing like a soft flute in the background; the rest of our thinking is like a brass band. When the brass band is playing we can't hear the soft flute. As soon as the band in our mind stops even for a second the flute-wisdom can be heard, because it never stopped playing in the first place.

Occasionally our brains scramble and suddenly we realize the way we've been seeing things doesn't seem to work anymore. Something goes "tilt" in our heads like a pinball machine. When this happens we may also get a flash of wisdom. Why? Because when our brains go "tilt," our head clears. This clearing allows wisdom to be heard. I am not recommending "tilt" as a way to hear wisdom but sometimes it happens that way.

Some people think if they meditate they will achieve a state of wisdom or higher consciousness. Some do, but others don't, so it is not necessarily true. This is because meditation is an act and a practice. Some people attempting to meditate get caught up trying to do the practice correctly, or they wonder what it will feel like when they reach enlightenment, or their minds are simply too distracted. Their thinking may still be running wild even while in the process of meditating, something one would think would slow down their minds. It is *the meditative state*, the slowing down of the mind, that is important, not the act of meditation. We can be in a meditative state with many things throughout everyday life. All the things people mentioned above are meditative for them. That is what counts.

A clear mind is something that happens within us; it is not something we do. Not only do we have a greater chance of hearing wisdom when the mind clears or calms, we also get a feeling of peace.

Jack Pransky

As I said to Diane [Chapter II] this feeling of peace is what most of us are really after in life.

If we take a step back and look inside ourselves we can see this really is the way we function. What we are looking for—peace of mind—is within us already. The pathway to peace of mind is a calm, quiet or clear mind—always. It is the same source and pathway from where our best ideas come.

If it is in us already, why don't we experience peace of mind all the time?

We inadvertently get in our own way.

We will always get unproductive or distracting thoughts. We can do nothing about that. But these thoughts will pass on their own—unless we do something with them or make something of them. It is not our thoughts that get us into trouble, *it is our thoughts about our thoughts that get us into trouble.*

We can have a thought such as, "I'd like to punch that guy in the face," but so long as we don't allow that thought to have power over us by taking it seriously we will not follow it. It will naturally flow out of our mind eventually, and that will be the end of it. If we get a thought, "I want to slug him," and then get another thought, "Go for it!" we give that first thought power over us and will likely follow it. If we have the first thought, but then have a thought of wisdom such as, "That's only a thought, and a ridiculous one at that!" we would catch ourselves and wouldn't follow the first thought. This process happens within us continuously and often too fast to recognize.

What we are talking about here is *our relationship with our thinking.* This relationship is far more important to our well-being than our actual thoughts. Without realizing it *we give thoughts power over us.* The alternative is to not take our thinking too seriously or to heart. Each is a different relationship with our thinking. We get to decide which relationship we want. Do we really want to be ruled by the same habitual thoughts we've carried with us for many years? Whichever we decide we'll experience the results.

If we want more peace of mind and wisdom in our lives, all we have to "do" is recognize when our minds are at peace, when our

40

wisdom speaks to us, and not accept what our thinking is telling us when we don't feel that way. When our mind clears, peace and wisdom appear.

It bears repeating again and again: *What we are looking for appears automatically when our mind clears.* There really is nothing we have to do to get where we want to be because *we are already there!* We are only in our own way with our very own thinking interfering with our intrinsic state of wisdom and peace, using our gift of Thought against ourselves.

C's Story

When C* first walked into my three principles/Health Realization training she looked quite insecure; the opposite of calm. She was very friendly with everyone and throughout the first day of training she engaged in numerous distracting side conversations. During the training she looked very confused, and at every break the first day she kept walking by me, shaking her head, saying, "I don't get it. I just don't get it!" That night or during the second day something happened to her. She seemed to relax. She walked by me again and said, "I get it now. I understand." The next time I saw her, a year or so later, C looked like a different person. She was attractive. She had lost a lot of weight. She had serenity about her. She had undergone a massive transformation.

I was living a pretty good life—living the best life that I thought was possible at the time. My job was going okay. I really enjoy working with kids in prevention and felt like I was pretty effective in working with my students. I was always a person who wanted to learn more; I wanted to be better at what I was doing in my life, personally and professionally. If there was any way I could be a better person I wanted to do it. So at age 29 I was a person searching for better ways of doing things.

Prior to that, I had a rough childhood. My parents were divorced when I was 4 or 5 years old. My mother was the primary caregiver for me and my sister, and we saw our father only occasionally. My childhood was not the best, and as a result I grew into adulthood being pretty insecure, thinking I was not a good person, I was worthless—just not feeling good about myself. So because of this I made a lot of poor choices, which led me into a lot of therapy. I was in and out of counseling most of my life.

I felt like I didn't feel good about myself because of the relationship with my mom. My mother would tell me I was

---

* At her request I am not using her name.

worthless and tell me she wished I was never born. So I grew up believing that I wasn't wanted. I never felt loved. I never was hugged or told "I love you," or anything like that. But I heard all the negative things that I did wrong over and over on a regular basis. My mom is a perfectionist—very high standards. I felt like I had to be perfect all the time, and any time I wasn't being perfect I was let to know I wasn't. Our house was to be immaculately clean at all times. If it wasn't, my mom got very angry. Every night she walked in the door from work, and if one slight thing was out of place she would go on a screaming rampage for the next two hours. So I always felt like I was on eggshells growing up.

One day when I was about 10 or 11 she came into our bedroom, and she was very angry at the condition our bedroom was in. She always thought it was an absolute mess. And so she started knocking things off our dresser—taking her hand and knocking things off—throwing things around the room, tearing sheets off the bed, screaming and yelling, and me and my sister are both crying, and she's throwing things around, screaming, telling us that we're pigs and we're lazy, and knocking the bed off the box spring. And she ran to the phone and said she was going to call the police to come get me and my sister (who was 6 or 7) because she couldn't take it anymore. And all I remember as a kid is just pulling on her and crying, tears streaming down my face, pleading with her, "Please don't call the police! We'll be good!"

So that was kind of my childhood. I wouldn't say that I was necessarily physically abused—I mean I certainly got hit, slapped across the face, hit where she could hit me, but I never had bruises left on me or anything like that—but I felt like there was a lot of emotional abuse.

Even though I felt that way about myself, I always felt like I was a person who had a lot of resilience—I felt like I'm going to get past this. I'm going to beat this. I'm a survivor. I'm not going to be miserable in my life because maybe some things haven't been perfect. I felt very driven. I'm going to go to college. I'm going to persevere. I was always thinking I was able to overcome better than my sister was. This happened, but I'm not going to let this hold me back. I want better for my life. I'm going to be somebody in life.

I learned from a lot of poor decisions. A big changing point in my life came when I was probably 24 or 25. I had been in a relationship with a man, and we had had a real rocky relationship. We dated for maybe two or three years, and we decided we needed to break up. It was a very, very, very unhealthy relationship—we were physical with each other at times, lots of verbal abuse. I truly thought that was the ending of that relationship. Later we got back together and I married him.

I started to go to therapy because I went into a very deep depression. A big turning point in my life was when the therapist referred me to a psychiatrist and I was put on Prozac. That was huge. That medication did wonders for me. It helped me move through my life in a way that I never had.

I had initially heard about Health Realization from [the director of a state prevention resource center], and she in a very slight way mentioned something to me and a couple of my colleagues that she had come across something called Health Realization. Again, I was one of those people who was always searching—I love to learn and I'm passionate about learning about different things, specifically anything related to social and mental health always fascinated me—so I was immediately curious. She said I'd be hearing about it and didn't really say anything else. Then I got invited to attend a Level I training at the state conference 2½ years ago.

When I came in I was very excited to be there. I felt like there was going to be something to this. When I first started hearing about this I said to myself, "What is up with this Jack guy? He's just sitting there so calm. He doesn't seem to have a lot of materials. What is this?" I mean, I was just completely puzzled. And that first day of going through it we're taking long breaks—what is up with this? Where is this going? But I felt like there was something to this, although everything was just completely puzzling me. I was trying to fit it into what I already knew about prevention, and

44

it wasn't fitting in. I was in complete confusion, and I was frustrated by my confusion. Yet Jack in front of me just seemed so calm and seemed to know something and see something that the rest of us were not seeing, and I wanted to see that.

That night I started reading *Modello*[*], and by the second day I started seeing some things. I remember seeing glimpses, starting to at least partially see what Jack was expressing in that training. I started to listen and watch the thoughts that I was having, and I thought, "Oh, my goodness! I have a lot of interesting thoughts go through my head." I started to notice what feelings were coming from my thoughts. So things were slowly starting to come for me. I was definitely seeing some things, and I was excited. And then after the training I did a lot of reading. Jack had given us a bibliography, and I probably read 80-90% of the books, and then the floodgates opened and, oh my God, I stated to see a lot of things. It was pretty amazing. I just kept having insights.

One of the big insights I had is, as I reflected upon my childhood and the way I was raised, I realized that I was believing all of the things that my mother had always told me. I believed that I was worthless. I believed that I couldn't do anything right. I believed that I would never amount to anything at times. And I believed those to be real. Then I realized that these were just thoughts in my head and they were not real; I was only making them real.

Then, never before in my life had I had such empathy for my mom. For the first time in my life I was able to see that the way I was raised and the way my mom acted towards me was her stuff. That had nothing to do with me. It was not personal. I mean, that was huge for me. It was never about me! It was all of her stuff, and that stuff was not true. I saw my mom with such different eyes. I felt sorry for her, where I had always been angry with her. It turned to: Oh my gosh, I feel so sorry for you. You must be in so much pain. Because if the thoughts that I was making up in my own head—if I

---

[*] Pransky, J. (1998). *Modello: A Story of Hope for the Inner City and Beyond.*

was in a low mood* and I was having low thoughts and I acted on those and I'm a person, my mom's a person, too, so she must have low quality thoughts. And if she has low quality thoughts, that's going to lead her to have certain feelings, and she's going to act on those feelings, and it's got nothing to do with me. It's got everything to do with her. That was huge. Huge!

It's so exciting—I've become so much of a less judgmental person. Prior to this I would say that I was a kind person, a good person, but I was pretty judgmental, too. Now I have a lot more patience with people. I'm able to understand people more. Because if I'm a human who functions this way, so is everybody else who I come in contact with. And that's really big.

Even with the medication I'd been put on before, I had never felt a peace and a calmness within myself. It was such an incredible feeling to know I already had this feeling inside of me; that everything I needed was already inside of me—I didn't have to do anything else. That led to so many things.

I used to be what I would call a "shopaholic." If I was feeling low, if I was feeling down, I thought the way to meet that need would be to go out and spend hundreds of dollars, then have my husband upset with me because I had charged up hundreds of dollars for clothes because I thought that would make me feel better. But it never did. If I had only realized that everything I need or I want is already in me—I just may have to wait a little bit for that feeling to come back, but it's already there.

Same with food. I think I was an emotional eater. If I was having a lousy day I would eat lots of food. I wanted to lose twenty-five to thirty pounds so badly, trying to work at it, trying to work at it. And when I realized that I didn't need any kind of food to make me feel better—everything I needed was already inside of me—this would bring about a calmness and a peacefulness. And saying, "I'm going to be okay no matter what." Just that, in and of itself.

---

* Note: I write about moods and their effects in Chapter VIII.

I also noticed the students I worked with—I always had a good relationship with them. I always enjoyed working with students, and I felt like they responded pretty well to me, but after this—I am not exaggerating—I could not sit in my office without a student being in my office at all times. I just felt like they were flooding to me, wanting to be around me all the time. Because I know that *I* was seeing them differently. I had always worked well with students, but even the kids who I used to say, Oh wow, this kid has a lot of problems—I was even seeing the kids with the biggest problems, that they're healthy too. If I had this innate health in me, so does everybody else in this world. They just let things get in their way too. When I saw that in them they started gravitating to me, just wanting to be with me, and I felt like I was more effective with them. I used to do a lot of talking at them, giving lots of advice, that didn't always make sense to me—I just felt like I had to say something— and it was almost like a burden was lifted off me. I didn't have to give advice anymore. I just listened, and my job became so much easier. I listened for their feeling. And I think they sensed that in me.

Prior to Health Realization I used to think that I had to work to be happy, that nobody's just happy. I would spend hours upon hours in self-help sections of the Barnes & Noble—because I wanted to be a good person, but what I missed was I already was. I already was, and I thought I had to strive to do that, and it wasn't all this work any more. You go to therapy and if you use these skills it will help you become a better communicator, and that's a lot of work. It gets real tiring after a while. And you get to a point where you do real well for a while, and then you drop down because that's a lot of work trying to keep that up. And for the first time in my life I didn't have to work to be happy. It was already inside of me. That's just incredibly freeing.

So everything around me just started to change, started to blossom and grow. And even now, even when I get down, most of the time when I go into a low period, or if I get into an argument, the intensity and the duration of anything that happens to me is cut in half to what it was before. I know that I'm going to be okay, and this is like solid grounding. I know that I will always be okay no matter what happens to me in my life, and that will never go away. You don't forget this. It's part of who you are. And this is who I am.

V. We Don't Have to Think Our Way Out of Our Problems

Tom held a high position in a high-profile business. He was fairly new to the company. When he first got his job his boss said, "Here's what we expect you to do..."

Tom said, "Fine."

Placed in charge of product marketing Tom began his job and performed extremely well. His boss praised Tom's work. When a new assignment arose his boss figured Tom could do it better than anyone else.

Tom said, "Fine."

Tom took on the new task too and again performed very well. Tom's boss sung his praises.

A few months later another new task came up. Tom's boss wanted someone he could count on. Tom came to mind.

Tom said, "Fine."

It happened once more. Suddenly it wasn't so fine.

Tom's day contained only a certain number of hours. None of his other tasks had been removed; only new ones added. Tom found he could not continue to do everything asked of him with the same quality. He simply did not have the time. He began spending more time after the workday ended. Even with the extra hours he felt less effective.

For Tom to take this job in the first place he had to move his family across the country and his nine year old daughter into a new school where she began having great difficulty. The local kids picked on her and bullied her. She felt desperately alone. She began to talk suicide. On top of that, Tom's wife and daughter did not have a very good relationship; the kid really needed her daddy. But because he put in so much extra time at work he couldn't be there with her. And because he put in so much less time at home his relationship with his wife began to deteriorate.

A little devil sat on Tom's shoulder shouting in his ear: "But you can do this! You can do it all and do it well if you just bear down."

Tom prided himself on the quality of his work. He had always been successful, no matter what company he worked for. Now he found himself unable to do well either at home or at work.

"How can I possibly solve this problem?" he asked himself. He began to bear down, analyze it, grind away. He got nowhere.

Tom came to me referred by a Three Principles counselor he saw where he'd lived previously. We met for an intensive session.

I asked an innocent question. Had he talked with his boss?

No.

Wouldn't it make sense to talk with the person who controlled his workload? How could anything possibly change if he didn't? Wouldn't wisdom say he needed to have a heart-to heart talk with his boss to try to come to a meeting of the minds? Didn't he need to draw a line in the sand (nicely, but firmly) about what he could and couldn't do for this company? What was his boss going to do, fire him? Doubtful. Obviously he was an extremely valuable asset to the company; his boss knew it or he wouldn't have assigned him all those tasks in the first place. Even in the unlikely event his boss did fire him over this, did he really want to work for a company with so little regard for his well-being? With Tom's track record lots of companies would love to have him. Tom could say to his boss, "I'd love to be doing all this for you beyond what I was originally hired to do, but it's hurting my ability to do any of the jobs well, and it's hurting my family."

Tom couldn't see it. His thinking didn't support it. He saw only a no-win situation. He had a hundred reasons why he couldn't talk to his boss. "I should be able to handle this." "It's not my place to tell a boss something different." "If I do this, what will the company think of me?" On and on. Meanwhile he was burning out rapidly and stressed beyond reason.

So long as Tom's head was full of what he knew, with all his analysis and processing, it was impossible for him to see the obvious or reach any new conclusions. He was paralyzed.

I said, "I don't care if you have a million excuses. Your little girl is suffering. If your family is suffering and your job is suffering I can't imagine the thinking that would make you not talk to your boss. I don't get it. Does this really make sense to you?"

This simple question caught Tom by surprise. He realized he had no choice but to talk with his boss. It was so obvious anybody could see it—except Tom. His mind had been too cluttered. The loud voices in his head had to cease for a moment. Tom had been working so hard to solve his problem based on what he knew that it clouded new insight. He realized if didn't get any satisfaction with his boss, then he had another decision to make, but the talk had to be step one.

Suddenly Tom fidgeted. He became extremely uncomfortable.

"What's going on, Tom?"

"I know I need to do it but I just can't bring myself to," he confessed. "I can't imagine actually going through with it." Despite what he wanted to do, his thinking hadn't changed.

I thought, "That's curious." Tom claimed to understand *the three principles* of Mind, Consciousness and Thought.[*] Intellectually he could rattle off their meanings perfectly, but intellectual understanding means nothing. I knew Tom was missing something big, but I didn't know what.

Something then occurred to me. "It seems like you just want things to get better on their own without having to change anything, even your thinking."

Tom stirred. Humbly, he admitted that was probably true.

I pressed: "There must be some fundamental, root belief that's keeping you from seeing the obvious here."

As soon as I said it he knew what it was. He held the belief, "If I can't do all this and hold it all together I'll feel like I'm a failure."

Bingo!

He could easily trace this thought to his upbringing. He'd picked up such thoughts from his parents. But his upbringing was over. He was no longer with his parents. Still he carried that belief with him like

---

[*] The Three Principles that create our experience of life—Mind, Consciousness and Thought—were introduced in the first two chapters. These principles are what this entire book is about

a yoke around his neck. Those thoughts were clogging his mind the way a sink drain gets clogged with gunk. Once he realized it was simply a bunch of thoughts he'd innocently picked up that only had as much power as he gave them, he felt more free. The drain cleared like in that old Drano commercial. The water flowed freely. He saw. He'd been a rat running on a wheel getting nowhere.

Often when we have a problem we become one of those rats. The rats don't get anywhere on the wheel because, looking in front of them, there's no apparent way out. The only way out is to step off the wheel sideways away from what the rat can see in front of it. In other words, the rat has a way out but so long as it is looking at what it knows it can't see the way.

This new perspective helped Tom step off the wheel. Instead of figuring out, analyzing, grinding away—all based on what he already knew, new perspective appeared in the form of wisdom. This allowed him to break out of his paralysis. His belief that everything would somehow work out on its own without taking any action was illusory thinking.

Hard work was Tom's modus operandi. He even talked about "working the principles" or "getting the principles to work for me." He made everything sound like work.

"The Three Principles are already working for you perfectly whether you realize it or not," I said. "You only need to relax and stop interfering with the free flow of them within you. Holding the beach ball under water is the work. Letting it go, allowing it to pop to the surface isn't work at all. You told me when you were on a recent trip to D.C. you just walked around the city having a wonderful time and feeling terrific for the first time in a long time. Was it work for you to feel healthy and have a clear head?"

The answer speaks for itself.

Sometimes it pays to work smart instead of hard.

An interesting thing happens when we have a problem. Our tendency is to try to figure it out, get to the bottom of it, process it, analyze it, sort it out. That is hard work and not helpful. We need fresh, new, clear ideas. We need new insights. We need wisdom to speak.

The way out of our problems is to step away from what we know, away from the noise and clutter so wisdom can be our guide. Our other option is to grind away and get nowhere.

Isn't it comforting to know we don't need to work to solve our problems? Isn't it amazing to know all that *trying* is exactly what *gets in the way* of a solution? Why? Because if we give up what we think we know—give it over to Mind, so to speak—we will get fresh, new ideas from this natural, infinite intelligence that speaks through us.

It's no different than losing our car keys. We can tear through our house, get more and more upset that we're not finding our keys, then after we've been through every drawer in our house and look in the same places again and again, we give up. When we give up we basically say, "I no longer know," and, boom, into our head comes, "They're in my pocket," or something like that. Trying to get to the bottom of something prevents us from getting to the bottom of it. It's one of the paradoxes of life.

When we have a problem, then, how do we get answers?

We could say something like, "I don't know how to solve this right now." "I don't know" is a great head-clearer (so long as people are truly okay with not knowing).

At the same time we know there is an answer somewhere. We have faith that there's an answer; we're just not seeing it right now. At some point, it will look obvious to us.

Then we *take it off our minds*, don't think about it, simply go about our business. Then when we least expect it, when our mind is calm, some solution will often pop into our head.

This may seem too passive. It seems we ought to be doing something more to get an answer and if we're not it seems as if we're slacking off, not getting down to business. It's often hard to trust it. Yet when I began to take my problems off my mind like this, my stress level plummeted. All the stress that came from trying to figure out what couldn't be figured out was no longer present in my life. Now I simply say, "I don't know, but I'd like to see an answer," forget about it, and go about my business. Now I get wise solutions with far less effort. When that stressful thinking dropped away I was left with peace.

If you don't believe this will work for you, realize you're not getting an answer by grinding away. Then see if this other way works.

When I was in my doctoral program I visited a fellow student who constructed a labyrinth in her back yard. I didn't really recall what a labyrinth was, so I asked her.

She said, "You ask yourself a question, then walk into the labyrinth, and by the time you come out the other side you get an answer to your question."

For readers who don't know what a labyrinth looks like, it's kind of like a maze but there are no false paths or dead ends. One path takes you around and around in circles in one direction, then you reach the center, then the path loops out in circles in the other direction. I thought it would be fun to try.

My father had very suddenly died about six months earlier, and my mother seemed to be in worse shape with each passing month. She wasn't responding to anything I or my siblings did or tried. We were at a loss. Nobody in our family knew what to do. We wanted to help her but we didn't have a clue. She wasn't able to focus, especially on what she needed to do for her life, how to get her affairs in order or anything. My brother and sister tried to help her sort through it all but it went in one ear and out the other. She was miserable. I was baffled. The more I thought about it the more lost I got. I couldn't come up with an answer.

This issue came to mind as I stood at the entrance to the labyrinth. I asked the question, "I'd like to know what can I do to help my mother through this," and I walked in.

I circled around to the left. Nothing.

I walked around and around. Nothing.

I reached the center. Nothing.

I began circling and spinning to the right. Nothing.

As I was about to step out of the labyrinth I heard a voice in my head.

It said, "Just love her."

Whoa!

"Oh my God," I thought. My head had been so cloudy I hadn't seen it. It was a shocking answer, but so obvious. One moment before, I could not have imagined this answer. I was amazed at myself: What could I have been thinking not to have seen this! But trying to figure it out never would have gotten me there.

I don't know how a labyrinth works but I suspect spinning in opposite directions scrambles the mind and clears the head. It's not the labyrinth that gives answers; the answers come from our own clear head. I never would have come up with that answer in a million years left to my analytical devices. But the voice was me. The answer came from me. And I didn't need a labyrinth to see it because the solution was there waiting to be seen.

Postscript: My mother now is doing great. She met a new companion and has a new life. She is as happy as she's ever been.

Julia is a Ph.D. psychologist from Puerto Rico. When growing up her alcoholic father sexually molested her repeatedly. For years she had been in therapy to heal that experience and feel good about herself, but she spent most of her life feeling depressed, not knowing how to live without depression. Recently she'd come out of an eight-year marriage. She worked very hard on herself, constantly.

She attended a Health Realization training that Gabriela Maldonado and I conducted there and discovered a missing link in her understanding of psychological functioning. Julia recognized the only thing keeping her from experiencing her innate health and wisdom was her use of Thought; that when she was not thinking unhealthy thoughts it would be there to guide her automatically. The idea comforted her.

"I need to work on seeing that in my life," said Julia.

Julia did some Spanish translating for me during the training, and Gabriela and I had a chance to spend a lot of time with her because she volunteered to take us around to see the sights. The three of us developed great rapport. Both Gabriela and I noticed how often Julia said she had to work on things—kind of like Tom, only Julia's hard work was on herself.

One day we traveled by ferry to beautiful Culebra Island off the coast. I sat with Julia, and Gabriela with Julia's ex-husband—they still got along well. While the other two were engaged in a Spanish conversation Julia asked me a question. Our conversation went like this:

Julia: I would like to know the difference between the kind of therapy I do and the therapy you practice using Health Realization.

JP: Well, I could attempt to explain it, but the only way it would really mean anything to you is if I showed you—with you playing the client. Would you be willing?

J: [slight hesitation] Yes. Okay.

JP: With Health Realization/Three Principles therapy, unlike in cognitive psychology, we are not interested in the content of one's thoughts. Instead we're interested in helping people see how they inadvertently use their creative power of Thought to make up things about themselves and others that are not helpful to them, and how people have a greater source of mental health and wisdom that sees through what they create with their thinking.

J: Can you give me an example?

JP: Okay. Once I went hiking in Arizona with a woman who told me she thought what was appealing to others about her was her keen intellect and her analytical mind and putting out how much she knew—and she knew a lot. But I didn't think that part of her was appealing at all. Instead, I liked the moments when she forgot all that stuff and her soft, vulnerable self came through. No wonder she found many of her experiences with others strained and unsatisfying. She came across hard because she'd been seeing herself through this false belief, which she had made up about herself. So I helped her see how she inadvertently used her thinking to make up a false notion about herself, which she then acted out of, and once she saw how she used her thinking against herself in this way, her soft, vulnerable, more appealing side automatically came out more, and her relationships became more satisfying. But that's not your issue.

J: What do you see is my issue?

JP: You think about yourself too much.

J: [laughs] You are probably right. Tell me more about that.

JP: If you weren't thinking about yourself you'd just be living, just being.

J: [sighs] I have worked so hard to try to get down to the bottom of my issues so I could feel good about myself.

JP: And where did it get you? You told me you've been depressed for many years.

J: [reflective] I know. But I also had some really good insights. I have the idea that the insights I've gotten through my life were the result of understanding what happened to me.

JP: It's great that you had good insights, but you were still depressed.

J: [sighs] I know.

JP: What if all those insights just came from your inner wisdom?

J: I know it does.

JP: Do you realize you keep saying "I know" to everything I say?

J: I know. That's because I really do know what you are talking about.

JP: We understand things at a certain level of consciousness, but the level you are seeing it at might only be on an intellectual level.

J: I know. [laughs] Ha! There I go again.

JP: That's good. You're seeing that now. You may not want to be so quick to say, "I know." You already know what you know. It's gotten you where you are in life. The idea is to go into "I don't know" to open yourself up to the new. It allows new insight to arise from the void. If you keep your mind filled with what you know, you don't allow that to happen. You could get more curious about what you don't see yet.

J: I realized just recently that there's a connection between my need to show that I know enough and my fear of loneliness. One time in therapy I connected that since I was a child I had to show that I know. I felt I had to do the schoolwork for my brother because we were in the same class and he wasn't able to keep up, and if he failed the grade I would be all alone. So in the bottom of it there's a fear of loneliness.

JP: Do you know you are never alone?

J: What do you mean?

JP: You are with your Self, with a capital "S."

J: [taken aback] I know all the good insights I have had through my life came through the inner wisdom of my Self. It's just that I forget and think that they come from all this effort and work I do.

JP: It's great to see that, but I don't think this is the main issue.

J: What is?

JP: I'm going to take a wild stab at this. You tell me if I'm wrong: You think the answers lie in the past.

J: [almost catches her breath] Yes, I do!

JP: Well, they don't. There is no answer in the past.

J: Aren't there some?

JP: There are none. Never. Zero. Zilch. Nada.

J: [frightened] Hold on, hold on here! Don't take that away from me.

JP: I seem to be striking a chord here. But I'm not taking anything away from you. I can't! I'm saying there are answers available to you but you're looking in the wrong direction. The past is over, dead, gone. The only thing keeping it alive in the present are your own thoughts.

J: But if I let go of the past what would be left? [pauses, taking a deep breath] Right now I feel this horrible knot, this feeling right here [points to her solar plexus] all the way through me. Looking to the past to sort out my problems is the only thing I know. I really do want to be stripped of that feeling, but it's all I know. Since I was a child, maybe seven to ten years old, I got the idea that what made me a good person, a good Christian, was as fragile as a glass that could be easily broken even when one was washing it. Maybe I also got this idea that living had to be difficult, that getting to be a good person implied having to work hard, like work hard on figuring out the past. [long pause] I have worked so much on myself. I know I have let go of many things of the past. I have gone through life feeling as if I have carried this army bag on my back full of so many negative experiences and feelings. It's much lighter today than ever, but it is still there. There are still heavy things there that are overwhelming and make me feel awful.

JP: What you're talking about now is just the past. What do you think would happen if you let go of that bag?

J: If I let go of the past? [pauses] I might have to feel happy. [smiles]

JP: You would be free. [The look on her face seemed to indicate what I said didn't quite register, but Julia later told me she was hearing something not from my voice but as if her inner wisdom was awakening and beginning to speak.] Do you hear me? You would be free. You would be *free!*

J: [touched, silent for a few moments] Why am I so afraid of freedom?

JP: You *are* free. You just don t realize it. If you weren't thinking fearful or depressed thoughts, you would automatically be free because you would be connected to your Health and wisdom. What's to be afraid of?

J: I just feel like there's this little person inside of me screaming, yelling, aching, suffering. It's something that many mornings does not even allow me to enjoy breakfast or work or life.

JP: Julia, that's just thought. [Again, I thought the power of what I was saying didn't seem to sink in.] That's *just* thought. That's just *Thought!*

J: [quite touched, now silent]

JP: You wanted to know the difference between traditional therapy and Health Realization/Three Principles therapy? That's an example right there. Many traditional therapies would try to figure out who and what this little person inside of you is and where it came from, unravel it, or think about it differently. In three principles therapy the only thing necessary is to truly see that this little person inside is merely an illusion created by your own thinking and it doesn't mean anything other than the power you give it (with another thought). You don't have to believe the messages this little person is screaming at you. If you didn't believe it you'd be left with your Health and wisdom—your spiritual essence. That's where your safety is. We are protected. Always.

J: I just feel I want to be on the other side, just able to let go of the feeling, ideas, fears—just go through the threshold and be free.

JP: You can be—and you will. These ideas you have about the past, they served a purpose for a time.

J: Oh, I am so glad to hear you say that. I thought you were discounting everything that I believed has kept me going.

JP: It helped you survive in the best way you knew how to do at the time. Those ideas served a purpose then. But now they have become a habit and are just interfering and separating you from your well-being, your wisdom, your spiritual essence. We inadvertently use our own thinking to create the illusion that we are separate from our spiritual essence. But we can't be. It's impossible. That illusory separation seems to be part of human nature. It causes all kinds of problems—with ourselves, in our relationships and all the problems in the world.

J: What you're saying is really comforting. I have always suspected that it shouldn't have to be so difficult. Our conversation gives me hope to be able to live life happily, knowing that for the first time I could be stripped of the feeling of sadness that accompanies the idea that everything has to be difficult. I could be stripped of the fear of happiness and freedom, and just be happy and free, just use my wisdom to guide me. That seems so much easier than all the hard work I've been doing.

That supreme paradox once again: Figuring it out, no matter how hard we try, gets in the way of an answer, which is why we're trying to figure it out in the first place. Once we truly realize this we fall into a state of grace about our problem. We become more grounded, centered, solid. We see the new. We find answers.

Julia began to see we don't have to think our way out of our problems or to happiness. Left to its own devices, unencumbered by our analytical thinking, wisdom shows the way.

After Julia's and my talk Gabriela offered this beautiful statement: "There's really nothing to fear. I'll go into fearful thinking from time to time, but I don't go into panic because I know I'm connected to an energy and a wisdom that's much greater than myself, and I know that energy and wisdom is going to keep me safe. So all these little events and situations we get afraid of –I know they won't be able to hurt my soul."

VI. The Feeling Is Everything, and It's Foolproof

When I first heard spiritual philosopher Sydney Banks say "the secret is in the feeling," or "the answer lies in the feeling," I had no idea what he was talking about. Now I do, or as much as I can see at this time. It is difficult to explain, so please bear with me here.

If in any moment we are feeling love or peace or joy or gratefulness or compassion or humility or humor, our mind is already engaged in a perfect state, doing everything it needs to do to experience this feeling. Even if we have no idea why we're feeling great, everything we need to know about what makes us feel great is already engaged inside us. Whenever our mind is functioning in that healthy way we experience the feeling of that state. In other words, whenever we have that feeling it means our mind is engaged and functioning exactly the way it needs to be. That's the secret! That feeling itself contains all the knowledge and wisdom we need know to get back to the same feeling!

If we were to look closely at our minds when we feel lousy we would see our mind working in a completely different way. We can see the difference in the way we're using our thinking. In habitual or low mood thinking we lose our good feeling. The emotion we feel as a result contains the knowledge and wisdom that our thinking is not on track, off base of our well-being, engaged in a way that is not serving us well. But when we're not experiencing the feelings we'd like, we need only see how our mind functions when we *are* feeling good, because at those times our thinking is already completely on course. So we already know how to get that nice feeling back. Our mind simply has to be engaged that way. The secret to how the mind works is embedded in that feeling.

I told you this would be hard for me to explain. Some readers might be thinking, "I have no idea what he's talking about, but something about it feels comforting." That feeling itself is enough! As soon as we struggle to figure it out what it means, our feeling drops. This in a nutshell is what I'm talking about.

At every moment we find ourselves at some level on a "well-being scale." Ten indicates the greatest feeling of well-being we could possibly imagine; one indicates the worst. There are many levels in between. At every given moment everyone is at a certain level on the well-being scale. So we could ask ourselves some questions:

What level on the scale am I at right now, in this moment?

At what level on this scale do I generally live my life? How does this compare with the level I'm at right now? If it is different now, what would make it be?

Am I generally living now at a higher or lower level than I often did in my past? Why?

What level am I usually in at work? Is there a difference between when I'm at work and when I'm living the rest of my life? If so, what would make it be that way?

Sometimes we're higher; sometimes lower but the big question is: What makes the difference? What is on our minds when we're at higher levels, compared with lower levels? How is our mind engaged when we're at higher and lower levels.

The answer to these questions points to the secret of how our mind needs to be engaged to give us the feelings we'd like, compared with the way it could be functioning. It is right there for us to see.

Airports are interesting places to observe people. Since 9/11 often the lines are longer than people anticipate and as flight time draws near many stuck in the long lines begin to worry. I watch many of them begin to panic and drive themselves into internal frenzy that leaks out for everyone to see. I feel for these people because I used to be the same way. Watching someone in one of these lines reminded me of something that happened to me ten or fifteen years before I became exposed to the three principles.

My car broke down. I live in rural Vermont and had to get back and forth to work, a commute each way of thirty minutes. I'd found a ride that morning, but that afternoon I couldn't find a ride home because I had to leave work early. So I hitchhiked. This did not concern me because after I'd graduated from college in 1968 I hitchhiked around the country by myself. Although it was the late '70s and things certainly had changed in the hitchhiking world, in Vermont they hadn't changed all that much. I caught a ride out of Montpelier fairly easily from some young hippie types, but after a while they had to turn off the main road so they dropped me off in the middle of nowhere.

The day could not have been more beautiful. It was one of those picture-perfect, crisp, clear, bright blue, sunny days in early autumn. As I stood on the road, thumb out, waiting for a rare car to come by I breathed in the beauty, face to the sun, head tipped back, eyes half-closed. I could not have been more content. For about ten minutes I stood in this state.

I then had the thought: "Uh oh, I've got to get home. I'd better bear down so I can get a ride."

My feeling changed instantly. Suddenly I was in a rush. I had to get home. I began to get agitated whenever a car passed.

Then another thought popped in. "Wait a minute! I'm not going to get home a second sooner whether I'm here worrying about not getting home on time or here enjoying this gorgeous day."

My feeling changed again. Suddenly I was as content as before.

Another five minutes passed. Another thought came: "Oh no, I've really got to get home! Come on, cars! Come on, people! This is getting ridiculous." I again became worried and agitated.

Then I remembered my previous thought. "But is worrying or trying to get there faster really going to get me there faster?" I laughed. As if wishing for it is going to make a kind driver come by. Again my nice feeling returned.

In the next ten minutes I could not believe how often my feelings changed. They changed each time I had a different thought! Though I knew I couldn't think myself to a ride faster I continuously fell into that same trap. Then I'd again realize its futility. Then I'd forget. Then

I'd remind myself again. Then I'd forget again. I astonished myself at the number of times this happened.

All the while the situation remained the same. I was stuck on the road without a ride and had to get home. My different feelings were caused by my different thinking, but which feeling would I rather live with? Which feeling indicated that I was in my Health? Wouldn't I rather wait for a ride (or anywhere, for that matter) in my Health? I saw my feeling in the moment, which I know now came from my own thinking, and I knew which feeling I'd rather live with.

I got home when I got home.

Lucky us, we have a foolproof, built-in mechanism that allows us to know whether our thinking is keeping us in low or high levels of consciousness: our feelings.

Our feelings and emotions are our ready-available guides. Their purpose is to tell us whether our thinking is on or off track of our Health and well-being.

If we feel anger or misery or depression or frustration or jealousy or guilt or fear—whatever the emotion—those emotions exist to let us know our thinking is off-base and *cannot be trusted*. When we feel low or mean, depressed or angry, worried or anxious, overexcited or fearful, we can't trust what our thinking is feeding us. As soon as we realize our feeling tells us we can't trust our thinking in that moment, we're suddenly in a position to listen to it or not, and our level of consciousness rises somewhat just by seeing it.

What about fear? Isn't the feeling of fear helpful?

Not in the way people usually think.

Many people say fear is helpful. For example, if I'm walking through the woods and a huge bear jumps in my path and I feel fear, in that instant it serves a useful purpose: Adrenaline kicks in and prepares my body for "fight or flight." In such circumstances fear certainly has a purpose—but only for a few moments.

Now suppose I act out of that fear. I may panic and do something stupid, possibly the exact opposite of what the situation calls for. While the fear-adrenaline connection prepared my body for action, if the bear doesn't run away and I try to flee or fight I'd probably regret it. I don't want to act out of fear. I want to act out of as much clear-headed wisdom as I can muster under the circumstances. If I'm feeling overwhelming fear I don't have my wits about me. I'd probably commit some knee-jerk act. So after the initial adrenaline-pumping, is fear helpful? I think not.

A feeling of fear cannot happen without a thought of fear, even though it usually happens so fast we would never even notice it as a thought. I realized this when we got a new little puppy—very cute—and I took her for a walk in the woods. As we were trotting along having fun Gypsy suddenly spotted a dark object in the woods. She got scared; the hair on the back of her neck stood up, and she began to slink down. What was going on? What was I about to confront?

It turned out a tree had blown over in a big storm and now lay on its side with its huge roots hanging half-way out of the ground, dangling like writhing snakes. Apparently Gypsy got spooked by a big dark fallen tree with roots.

I realized dogs too apparently learn what to fear; what they specifically fear is not instinctive. Instinct is how they react—hair standing up on neck, slinking down, etc.—but what creates the fear is not instinct. It may be instinct that they fear big, dark objects, but they somehow have to interpret whether the big dark object is harmful. Gypsy must have had a dog-thought that the dark object meant "danger!" It's tough to think like a dog, but what's obvious is if she didn't have a scary thought she never would have feared a tree lying on its side. It's the same for humans. Fear is always preceded by a fearful thought because we have to perceive fear in the first place.

About six months before we got Gypsy one day I took a walk in the same woods, turned a corner and in fact did see a bear. Fortunately the bear was more scared of me than I was of it because it took off running unbelievably fast. They say a bear can outrun a horse for short distances, and any doubts I ever had about that were immediately dispelled. If that bear wanted to come after me I wouldn't have stood a chance because my reaction time would have been far too slow. Lucky me, the bear took off in a different direction. When I first saw the bear

I had a momentary feeling of fear. Adrenaline pumped instantly, and my body readied itself.

Though it wouldn't have helped much in this case I'll concede that adrenaline allows us to muster the resources for whatever we need to do, which serves a necessary purpose. Fear is meant to take care of us in that way. Suppose, however, the next time I wanted to walk in the woods I had the thought, "Uh oh, what if I run into the bear again, and what if it is not so accommodating next time?" Actually, I did have that thought, but I didn't take it seriously and went for a walk anyway. Had I taken that thought seriously I would have been fearful all over again without having stepped foot in the woods. Here I would be, safe in my house, in fear, adrenaline pumping through my body—my body is all prepared now—and the bear isn't even around. Does this make sense? If I took that feeling seriously I might not walk in the woods ever again. (Thank God Vermont doesn't have grizzlies.)

After the initial flash of fear-pumping adrenaline the fear no longer serves us. No matter what our emotion—fear, anger, jealousy, anxiety, depression, worry, etc.—it always reaches a point where we need to ask ourselves, "Is this serving me well?"

What about anger? Isn't anger a worthwhile and necessary feeling? Again, not in the way most people think.

In some situations it looks as if anger is justified. If someone comes along and steals my money many people would say I should be angry. But anger is not a given. Anger happens *based on how we see it*. If I happen to think, "My goodness, what could a person be thinking to interfere with somebody's life like that, to have no regard for others? That person must live in a horrible world to be able to do that to someone," I would not feel anger. I would feel something akin to compassion. Anger comes from the way we see it, from the way we think it. [More on this in Chapter VIII.]

Does anger get my money back? No. Does being miserable get my money back? No. Does compassion get my money back? No. Either way I don't have my money. But I'm the one who has to live with my feelings. They're mine. Which feeling would I rather live with?

Some say anger motivates us to take action. So suppose out of my anger I go off screaming to the police and demand they find this guy. Or out of my anger I shake down anyone who happens to pass by to see if they took the money. I'm certainly motivated, but would those actions be constructive? Instead of anger I'd rather have wisdom be my motivating force. I'd rather have wisdom guide me in what to do. When anger is present wisdom is blocked; it can't get through. I'm in my own way.

How do I know when my wisdom is speaking and not my anger? It has a different feeling attached. It is quiet, calm, solid, certain. The feeling is foolproof. It always tells me which thoughts to listen to.

The feeling is like a traffic light. A yellow-light feeling (in this case, annoyance) means our thinking needs to slow down, proceed with caution—we'd better take a step back and see what's going on. A red-light emotion (in this case, full-throttle anger) means stop, our thinking simply can't be trusted—time to regain our bearings and calm way down. A green-light feeling (in this case, feeling compassion or "it'll work out okay") means our thinking is on track of our Health— go ahead. I'd probably still report it to the police, but with the right feeling. It will be heard better.

When we use our feelings as signals this way our feelings seem to change. They rise. We feel better, more centered, wise. That we can trust!

When we trust what the feeling tells us, we're safe, because we know we don't have to follow our thinking to our own detriment.

Sometimes we miss what our feelings tell us because we get so used to the feeling it seems normal. This happens most often when overtaken by ingrained habits of thinking, where without knowing it we often use our thinking against ourselves. Sometimes we can even sacrifice our own well-being for an illusion. Take people I affectionately call "absorbers." By this term I don't mean to put anyone in a box; I only mean I've noticed a bunch of people with a similar thinking pattern. These are people who put others ahead of themselves, which is a beautiful thing, unless it is to their own detriment. Tom, for example [Chapter V], absorbed everything thrown his way at work to his detriment despite his feelings telling him not to trust this thinking. Most others I've met are women who think they have to absorb everything their male partner does and take responsibility for maintaining the relationship, keep it on an even keel no matter what, allegedly for the good of the relationship or their family's peace of mind or for what they think (erroneously) is their own peace. Despite the low feeling it brings it is easier not to rock the boat.

Josephine absorbed that her partner smoked pot all the time and didn't seem to have ambition to find a job. Although when they first met she found it endearing because she admired his freedom, over time it began to rankle. She was the one who had to ensure enough money came in, and not enough did. She began to drop subtle hints. He didn't take them. Yet she wanted to see the best in him. She wanted to see his Health; she didn't want to see problems. Besides, to tackle it head on would rock the boat of their relationship, and they had a good relationship. Thus, she had to take the responsibility to maintain the relationship for the good of the relationship—or so she thought. If she forced the issue she didn't know what would happen. Fear took over. So she just took it, absorbed it.

Tina's partner was strapping, athletic, good-looking and intelligent. His only problem was he couldn't seem to get his life together. He worked so hard getting nowhere it completely stressed him out. Sometimes he fell into deep depression. She couldn't pull him out. Yet she stuck with him because he needed her; he might not be able to make it without her. She did this despite becoming increasingly unhappy and losing herself in the process. She absorbed the pain for his sake.

Anne's husband did not get along very well with her teenage kids from a former marriage. One of his sisters, who lived in the Caribbean, had become a crack addict, gave birth to baby, couldn't take care of her, was thrown in jail, and none of her relatives there would have anything to do with her. Her little girl was about to be sent to foster care. Anne's husband wanted to take in his sister's kid—a noble gesture on his part—but Anne knew all responsibility for this child would fall on her, because all responsibility in the household always fell on her. She told him she didn't want to do it. This was a crack-cocaine baby who would likely require a huge amount of attention and care, plus Anne was afraid of the effect it might have on the rest of their children. Her man insisted. Anne absorbed it. As predicted he took little responsibility for this child's care; it all fell upon her. As the girl grew older and went to school she began to show severe behavioral problems. She started to torture their youngest boy. Anne wanted to send her for a mental health evaluation; her husband would not hear of it. The girl's behavior began to drive Anne crazy. She had little energy to devote to the rest of her kids. Her relationship with her oldest daughter began to deteriorate. Anne began to get sick frequently. It affected her work. She had thoughts of suicide; it seemed the only way out, except she couldn't because of her other children. Still, she refused to tell her husband she couldn't handle it any more, absorbing it all for the good of the relationship.

Behind "absorbers" is faulty thinking that says, "I'm the one who has to sacrifice myself. I'm the one who must take all responsibility." This thinking is an illusion that looks like reality.

How can we tell? *Something doesn't feel right.* A healthy relationship feels good to both parties. A healthy relationship is not absorption by one, not a sacrifice of one. A healthy relationship is coming to a meeting of the minds when there is a difference of view, a difference of satisfaction between the two. A healthy relationship is a two-way affair. How can we tell? Whether our feeling is right! Again, the feeling is foolproof.

What if someone doesn't know what they're feeling? How can the feeling be used as a signal?

Do we feel fine or lousy? That's all we need to know.

Some say, "I just feel numb. I don't feel anything." I would say "numb" does not fall within the "feel fine" range, so numb means we're having faulty thinking that can't be trusted.

Do we need to know specifically what we are thinking to make us feel lousy?

No. If I'm feeling lousy, so long as I know it is coming from my own thinking and not from the outside world, that I am the one thinking up lousy thoughts for some reason, that my thinking is off-base and can't be trusted, that knowledge seems to be enough to take the power out of the emotion.

Speaking personally, sometimes I do find it helpful to know what my specific thinking is. I love when hidden thinking gets revealed to me, when I see a blind spot. The more this thinking is brought into the light the less it controls me, such as when I was not at peace writing my dissertation. This may appear to be a contradiction, but it isn't.

What I do not find helpful is to search for the hidden thinking or the blind spot, because the search is often futile and leads to frustration. This is because we're searching with our analytical minds, the very mind that created the blind spot in the first place. In this case, the purpose of our analytical mind is to protect the blind spot and keep it hidden.

Instead of searching or analyzing, our hidden thinking or blind spots naturally reveal themselves when we are ready to see them. Pardon me for this example, but if we're constipated we can push and strain as hard as we can and not much will happen except hemorrhoids. Or we can relax, go about our business, eat healthy and wait for the release when it is ready. It may not come any faster. It may be just as uncomfortable. But at least we won't be adding to our burden, putting more stress on the system. (Sometimes graphic examples help drive a point home.)

If we really want to discover our blind spots and possibly speed up the process we could ask (of Universal Mind), "I'd like to see why I'm feeling this way." Then forget about it. An answer is more likely to come when the mind is quiet.

Sometimes the feeling feels so real it affects us physically. Neurobiologist Candace Pert, author of *Molecules of Emotion* attests to this. As a New Englander I am a die-hard Red Sox fan. With all other Red Sox fans I had been frustrated my entire life. So in the 2004 season when they were down three games to none in the American League Championship Series to the dreaded New York Yankees (who always won), and the Red Sox won the next three games to tie the series, I got excited. In the final game Derek Lowe had been pitching a great game and the Red Sox were ahead by a few runs when the manager, Terry Francona, took him out of the game and put in the great but tired Pedro Martinez, who had given up more runs than usual in his last couple of outings. I couldn't believe it! I thought this was about as stupid a move as when last year's manager kept Pedro in too long in the final game when tired, and the Red Sox lost that series (to the Yankees, of course). "No!" I screamed at the TV. I was sure this was an omen. They were going to blow it again! They always did. The first batter got a hit off Pedro. My heart started to pump hard. I could feel a tightness across my chest. The second batter got a hit. "Oh no!" I was absolutely certain the Red Sox would lose. The tightness turned into pain. I remembered former President Clinton had a pain in his chest and he ended up with heart surgery. I was so certain the Red Sox would lose that the pain became too great. I couldn't take it any more. I actually had to leave the room and go to bed. This feeling had nothing to do with my thinking, of course; this was real! Or so I thought.

Of course it had everything to do with my thinking! As soon as I left the TV and resigned myself to the fact that the Red Sox would lose again the pain in my chest subsided. I woke up the next morning and found the Red Sox had won. Judy, meanwhile, had a great time watching the Sox win and teased me unmercifully. But, miraculously, the pain in my chest disappeared completely and didn't return. I'd gotten so wrapped up in the thought that they were blowing it again and what this meant to me, that I thought the Red Sox were doing it to me, personally. I forgot I was doing it to myself. I'm the one who decided it was important that the Red Sox won. It is just a baseball game! I'm the one who decided that they were going to lose (and since they didn't, that illusory thinking is obvious). I'm the one who decided I couldn't take it anymore, and it caused me to miss the win and celebration I had been waiting for my whole life. I'm the one whose thinking caused my "Oh no!" feeling and the tightness in my chest. I was so caught up in it I did not see it as my own thinking. My emotional feeling, of course, all the while was screaming at me to see it.

71

Thank goodness the Red Sox ended up winning the World Series. I can rest easy now.

Every time we feel an emotion such as anger, frustration, stress, jealousy, guilt, anxiety, worry, fear, depression, we are at a fork in the road. One path of the fork is to see this emotion as coming from the outside world; that is, somebody doing something to us or something about our circumstances. The other path is to see the emotion arising from our own thinking, from ourselves.

So long as we believe our emotion is coming from the outside world we're stuck feeling that way until the outside world changes.

When we see our emotion coming *from our own thinking*, we know it will dissipate when our thinking changes because our thinking always changes eventually. If we know we're the one making up the emotion, we get to decide which feeling we would rather live with.

As Yogi Berra says, "When you come to a fork in the road, take it."

Picture our Health as a ball of pure white light within us, with the center of that light containing and emanating pure love. As the light extends further and further from its center it loses an increasing amount of its purity and brightness and gradually becomes darker, more dense. If a measuring stick emanated from this center of light and extended all the way out to our darkest space we could (figuratively) measure the distance of how far away each feeling or emotion is from this center of pure love.

In other words, if we are so totally depressed and in despair that we feel suicidal, our measuring stick would tell us we are about as far away as we can get from pure love and Health.

If we feel sorrow, we are still far away, but the distance from pure love/Health is slightly less.

If we feel some sadness, the distance is less still. If we feel only a touch of sadness, it is less still. [Note: I'm not saying it isn't natural to feel sad when, for example, someone close to us dies. Of course that is natural! That sadness can do us no harm—if we allow it to flow in and flow out as it will without assigning meaning to it. Yet some people begin to live in sorrow, and it defines their lives. The natural sadness becomes corrupted and is now detrimental. At a certain point, continued sadness stops serving us well.]

If we have a bittersweet feeling, the distance from our Health is less still.

If we feel okay about whatever happened, it is less still.

If we feel relief, the distance is less still.

If we feel humility or compassion, it would be less still. Now we're getting pretty close to love and Health.

If we feel joyful or grateful, we may even be closer to Health.

If we feel unconditional love or pure peace of mind, we are perhaps as close as we can get.

This is the measuring stick. I wonder if that is what John Lennon meant in the song "God" when he sang, "God is a concept by which we measure our pain."

We could place anger on that vertical same scale, from total outrage and fury to downright anger, to irritation, to mild annoyance, to feeling neutral, to feeling okay, to feeling compassion, to feeling the peace or love that is our Health. We could do this with any feeling or emotion. There are possibly infinite levels.

The only difference between a lake with waves and a lake without waves is the wind. A lake would be calm except for the wind. We would be calm if not for our thinking. We can tell how much of a turbulent effect the wind has on the lake by the size and strength of the waves. We can tell how much effect our thinking is having on us by the size and strength of our feelings.

The wind is invisible. We can only feel the effects of it. Most of the thinking that affects us is also invisible. Our feelings are the only thing that tells us something is amiss.

Most important is to continue to realize that the feeling we want is already within us. It is only hidden, obscured by our own creations of thought. We already have what we're looking for.

Monica's Story

During a break on the second day of a Three Principles training I saw Monica standing in a daze, her face all flushed. I went up to her and asked what was going on. She told me she just had a huge revelation and felt very weird, completely different, as if a surge of energy just whooshed through her body. At that moment I knew Monica would never be the same. This is how she told it:

I see life much different than I did a few days ago, but to describe my life as I see it now wouldn't make much sense, so I will first address how I saw my life before I attended the Health Realization workshop.

When I was growing up my parents were migrant workers, they moved with the seasons. I was born in Ohio, but I only lived there three days. My first educational experience occurred at a Spanish Head Start. This was the place I believe I learned that my upbringing was not one which was acceptable to society. Granted, our living conditions were not the greatest, but what impacted me more was the festering of unhealthy beliefs, thus behaviors. My father was incestuous, and many of our neighbors were child abusers.

When I was seven my mom left my dad after she received a blow to the womb, killing my sister. However, my mom leaving my father did not stop the negative occurrences in my life. My backpack of negative life experiences kept getting heavier. After my dad was gone the sexual abuse continued with my mom's boyfriends, a stepfather and some neighborhood teenagers and adults—not just men, but predominantly. (I don't know what the statistics are on poverty and unhealthy behaviors, but in my situation they seemed to walk hand and hand.)

As a teenager I felt burdened by this weight and sought any means to forget for a while. This steered me to more unhealthy situations (crime, drugs, etc.). At sixteen I found myself pregnant, weighted by the backpack of abuse and the pregnancy, my body began to naturally purge itself of the toxic backpack. I began to experience flashbacks. When I was pregnant with my daughter I tried to count all the times I had been sexually abused—I stopped at twenty and asked what the point was. I began to experience memory lapses, and phobias. I went to therapy and learned how to handle/live with my side effects. I married my child's father and was with him for six years before I figured out I was in an abusive marriage. I walked away from my marriage knowing I no longer wanted to be belittled, hit and degraded. I just wanted to be me. What I didn't realize was I also walked away believing I was the type of person who drew abusive people.

Thus I began dating a guy a year after I divorced, and I went from a bad situation to a much scarier situation. After some violent outbursts I went to the court system in hopes of protecting my family from the threats he made towards their safety. I obtained a restraining order, which enraged him, and he violated the order. He was released on conditions, which he also violated. The police officer I spoke to about the last violation informed me he could not do anything about the situation and for me to contact the State's Attorney the following day. I ended up going to the police station to file a statement. While I was running around trying to get him arrested, he broke into my mother's house (where I lived) and waited. My mother made it home before I did, and he kidnapped and raped her.

The long judicial process took its toll on me. A grueling eight hour deposition left me feeling dirty, wrong, guilty, overall a complete fuck-up. It took five long years for this man to be sentenced, while I continued to receive letters from him threatening my family's and my safety. When the defense attorneys said I had invited him into my mother's house to set her up, I couldn't even defend myself, and I begged the judge to allow me to go home. He was never convicted of the rape; they couldn't prove that the evidence left in my mom's bed wasn't caused by me. (They made it look like I had sex with him in my mother's bed and that was why there was semen and hair samples in the bed. But I never slept with him in my mother's bed.) So he was convicted only of the kidnapping, breaking and entering, and assault.

My mind was not doing the greatest—my backpack had now become a rucksack covering the length of my body. The contents of this rucksack contained messages to me, a few of which were: I was tainted from birthmark to receive the wrath anyone chose to bestow on me. (Why else would a father hurt their child?) I asked for what I got from this world. I was inadequate—I was lacking something. I didn't have what it takes to be good enough. And now I had exposed my family to a man that caused them harm.

Education, therapy, meeting great people, my children, and (not to forget) my innate health helped me endure my heavy rucksack. It was not until a few days ago did I discover that I could remove, no, rid myself, of the rucksack. No, I didn't figure out how to erase my memory—actually something much better. I realized I wouldn't want to. I like who I am and without my experiences I wouldn't be who I am today.

This insight came to me as little tidbits from conversations that took place during the Health Realization workshop, but the huge void was filled when our presenter brought in a recovering heroin addict to tell her story, and she said that while she would like to free herself of needing pot, she had smoked it the night before. She said she didn't have to be perfect or judge every little occurrence in her to represent who she was. She wasn't going to beat herself up over it. The kindness I saw her offer to herself served as a catalyst to the thought that my past only had a hold on me because I was allowing it to, through my thoughts.

My second thought was that I had created my reality of my past, and I had the ability to re-create it. This thought led to a euphoric feeling of empowerment. This changed the way I saw my life. I suddenly realized I didn't have to carry around the rucksack, but rather I was choosing to. Many emotions rushed at me all at once when I realized, "I am healthy. I am perfectly okay as I am.," and it's only when I imagine I'm not that I move further away from the truth. I even feel different about my perpetrators. It was like fifty years of weight had been taken off my tired shoulders. That weight has never returned.

So where has this realization brought me? To a different level of living. Before, I was trudging through life. Now I actually enjoy it! My current relationship with my partner has grown in leaps and bounds. He was the first person I flung my new knowledge at, and to both of our surprise, he got it! We spend more time truly listening to what the other person is saying. We listen with an open heart. I cannot describe in words what was blocking our relationship from being healthy other than we weren't in our health.

My job has been testing this newfound awareness every day, and every day not connecting to my innate health seems more like a struggle. My eyes and heart have become open. And even though I want to tell the world, I know I first need to continue to live in my health and by doing so others will join the journey. I also feel different about [my former boyfriend]. Do I want to run into him on the streets? No. But I no longer fear him. (He is currently trying to get out of jail because of hepatitis.) I feel more a sense of sadness that his eyes and heart are not open. Water under the bridge. If I hold grudges I feel terrible; if I see it as innocence then there is no one to hold a grudge against.

Overall in my life I feel strong (I could tackle anything), calm (my mind only races when I doubt myself), at ease, whole, pride, a love for myself, and an optimistic outlook on the world. Thanks for showing me what I have always known and felt but couldn't quite believe until I saw it in someone else.

Jack Pransky

VII. What We See is What We Get

In my book, *Prevention from the Inside-Out*[*], Lisa (from Chapter I) told the story of how from the moment her daughter was born she saw her as a manipulative little brat.

Her daughter Bridgett whined and cried from the beginning. Before long Bridgett screamed all the time. She appeared to be writhing in agony. After six months Lisa discovered her daughter was allergic to her breast milk. This explained the pain and crying. Lisa switched to soy formula and got instant relief—two or three days of peace, until Bridgett cut her first tooth and got her first ear infection. The screaming began again. From that time on she had a series of teeth cuttings and ear infections—more crying and screaming. Soon Bridgett learned to cry to get what she wanted. Lisa felt she never had a chance to bond with her daughter; she was too busy fighting the manipulation and brattiness.

One day in a long-term professional Three Principles training Lisa complained about her daughter and their relationship. On the surface it seemed to most that she needed better parenting skills. I heard a more fundamental problem. The main problem was how Lisa *saw* her daughter. For seven years she saw a manipulative, conniving little brat.

I asked, "Lisa, do you think your daughter could possibly be seen in any other way?"

Dripping with sarcasm she said, "Oh yeah, I'm going to see my daughter as a sweet, precious little thing."

Suddenly an image flashed before her. She pictured Bridgett throwing a temper tantrum in the middle of the floor. Lisa had been attributing the reason for the tantrum to the fact that Bridgett was a

---

[*] Pransky, J. (2003). *Prevention from the Inside-Out.* Bloomington, IN: Author House.

manipulative brat. Lisa then realized, "Oh my, I am making up the reason my daughter is having a temper tantrum. Like I was making up that she didn't want me when I didn't know she was allergic to my breast milk. I don't really know why she's doing this."

Lisa then had a monster insight: "Oh my God," she gasped, "I am making up who my daughter is! I am creating an illusion that my daughter is a manipulative brat, then I'm acting toward her *as if* she really is."

Lisa cried. She suddenly saw a different child.

With Lisa's revelation everything changed. When she arrived home she apologized instantly to Bridgett. From that moment on they have had a wonderful relationship.

The only thing that changed was Lisa's thinking, from, "She's a manipulative little brat" to, "I'm making up who she is."

Whatever illusion we see is exactly what we get. If we see a manipulative brat, we get a manipulative brat. Consciousness takes that thinking and makes it look so real. When we see an illusion for what it is, however, new possibilities instantly arise. We realize we could make up *anything* about who our kids are, as well as everyone and everything else. It's all up for grabs. Anyone can look differently to us. Any situation can look different. Each level of consciousness presents a different lens through which we see. We're the ones who create the lens.

All we need to realize is whoever or whatever we're seeing in the moment is coming *from us.* It's not them! Simply seeing this already alters what we see to some extent, because we have greater perspective. When we see the illusion we are no longer stuck with the "reality" we see and an entire world of possibilities opens before us. Nearly infinite possibilities abound, yet we inadvertently pick one to see at any given time. If we realize this range of vertical possibilities in every moment, however, we have the opportunity to take whatever we see a little less seriously than we normally would. New worlds can open before us, as they did with Lisa.

Lisa couldn't stop having occasional thoughts such as, "My daughter's manipulating me" or "She's being a brat." However, now when this happens she knows it is only a habit of thinking that's kicked in, especially in a low mood. Like John Nash in the movie, *A Beautiful Mind*, she is able to turn her back on—not believe—that kind of thinking. Even when Nash realized he was creating paranoid schizophrenic illusions, he could not stop them; he still saw them. His turnabout came the moment he realized the kid he was seeing over the years had not aged. Suddenly he saw the illusions for what they were. Suddenly Nash knew he was the source, the creator. Suddenly he realized he did not have to believe them as real; therefore they no longer had to rule his life. So while he couldn't stop them, *he could turn his back on them.* We all have the same power. Lisa, too, stopped taking those thoughts seriously and saw a "new" Bridgett.

On a hike in Manuel Antonio, a beautiful Costa Rican park off a wonderful beach, we were told if we arrived early enough would likely see some monkeys up in the trees. For a long time I didn't see any. I didn't care; I thought the park was gorgeous. I was having a great time hiking in the beauty. Someone stopped me on the trail and asked if I had seen any monkeys. He hadn't and was really annoyed at this, as if it was some kind of personal affront.

Different thinking, different experience. What we see is what we get.

Eventually I did see some very cute little monkeys. It was icing on the cake.

Remember in Chapter VI when we talked about whether anger was necessary? What if we were subjected to sexual abuse or were raped? If we look closely, we still could have a wide range of emotions.

If we look back and say, "It ruined my life." That level of consciousness, based on our thinking, would give us the experience of a ruined life.

If we say, "I'm damaged goods," we get a life experience of being damaged.

If we think, "That was terrible, but it's not going to ruin my life," from that level of consciousness we experience being okay.

81

If we say, "Wow, I really learned something from this; this makes me know to be more vigilant and take more care," we would be seeing at yet a different level and would experience a different feeling.

I'm not saying what happened isn't a terrible thing and the perpetrator doesn't have to pay. I'm not saying one level is better than another. I'm not saying we should be seeing the experience in any particular way. I'm only saying we're the ones who get to live with the feeling determined by whatever level of consciousness we see it at, and that becomes how we experience it. We're the ones creating our own levels.

Gabriela taught a Health Realization class at Juvenile Hall in San Jose, California. The class met once a week for an hour-and-a-half. After holding the class for about four months, one day she walked into class and something seemed amiss. Usually when she and her co-trainer, Celestine, came into the room the kids immediately settled. This day they were already sitting in silence. You could cut the tension with a knife. Over the months they'd established nice rapport with the group. This felt different.

Gabriela glanced around the room and saw five new kids in class. Many kids wore gang tattoos on their arms and chests, but one new kid more aggressively displayed a gang tattoo just above his eyebrows—right in your face. He seemed extraordinarily intense. Gabriela sat directly across from him, facing him, so she could watch him. Next to Gabriela sat a rival gang member. She noticed the kid with the forehead-tattoo staring directly at him, eyes glaring, intense, aggressive, staring him down, never looking away.

The trainers began introductions and, as always, tried to keep it light. They started with those who'd been in group a while, asking as they introduced themselves to name their favorite food. The kids willingly participated—until it came to the new kid who continued his bold stare.

"My name is Jose," he grunted, "and I've got nothing else to say." Period.

Celestine, sitting next to him, tried to encourage him to talk. He wouldn't. Tension built. The more Celestine tried the greater grew the tension. Jose stared at her with evil eyes, then shifted his stare to Gabriela sitting across from him.

For the first time since this class began Gabriela felt a surge of fear. She looked him in the eye for a second, then looked away at the floor. His energy was too powerful, too unnerving. Something seemed about to blow.

She heard a voice within her. "You have to look him in the eyes."

She didn't want to, but she looked up and stared back at him firmly. Staring contest. Gabriela thought it would last forever. Jose eventually looked away.

At session's end Gabriela considered calling the guards to remove him from the group. Another inner voice said, "Wait and see."

Jose came in the next week with the same intensity. She tried to joke with him, but he'd have none of it. "We should have had him removed," she thought. "I'll deal with it after class."

Celestine always brought cookies for the kids. This week they were wrapped individually and soon the wrappings were scattered everywhere. Gabriela saw an opening. Nonthreateningly she approached Jose.

"Can I ask you a favor?" she asked him sweetly.

"Okay."

"Would you mind picking up everybody's wrapper and throwing them away?"

"Sure, ma'am," he said.

Gabriela was shocked. "Thank you, Jose."

She sat next to him now, teaching the class. Other kids were talking, making noise.

"Hey," he said, "Give her some respect! She's trying to teach."

Gabriela nearly fell off her chair.

She turned to Jose and said, "Thank you."

Jose then began to listen. He listened to her teach about Thought. He listened to her say everyone has Health and wisdom inside them.

At the end of the class as everyone got up to leave, Gabriela said, "Thank you, Jose. See you next week."

Time passed. In class they talked about Mind, Consciousness and Thought. Jose said he suddenly understood how everyone was making up their own world. He had a profound insight. Gabriela could see it in him physically. When the class was ready to end Jose asked if they could stay ten more minutes. He seemed really interested. In subsequent classes Jose even began to teach others.

"I know I'm making this up," he said. "It's not the counselor."

He started softening. He began smiling. Suddenly he had dimples. Before, his face was full of such aggression and rage Gabriela had missed his face completely and saw only the rage. She now noticed he was a beautiful kid.

"Oh my God, Jose, you have dimples!"

Jose smiled.

"Who would have thought that this bad, tough, ugly-attitude kid had dimples!" she said to him.

Jose smiled more. "I had to pretend to be tough because I was uncomfortable," he said, "but when I started feeling comfortable I could let that go."

"Yeah," Gabriela said. "Sometimes we create funny beliefs about being tough and about ourselves. Do you want to talk about beliefs?"

"Yeah," said Jose. "Beliefs are something you stand by and you die for."

"Well, that's a funny belief about beliefs," Gabriela said.

Jose reacted. "What do you mean?"

By now Gabriela felt a loving, strong bond between them. "Well, what's really a belief?" she asked.

The kid next to him piped up, "A belief is a thought."

Jose growled, "No, it's not a thought!"

When Jose talked, he commanded respect. All the other kids shut up and listened. He was higher up in the gang. Other kids didn't refute him. But one of them said, "Well, it kind of has to be, because you cannot start a belief without a thought."

"No, no!" Jose said, irritated.

Both kids looked at Gabriela. All the kids now looked at Gabriela.

She said, "Actually, he's right, Jose. A belief is nothing more than a thought."

Pointing aggressively to his tattoo Jose said, "Do you mean to tell me that hundreds of people have died because of a thought!"

"Yes."

"You need to shut up! Just be quiet. I can't hear about this any more."

Gabriela said, "Okay."

The group sat silent for a few moments. Jose stared at the floor.

He took a deep breath and looked up at Gabriela. "Okay, tell me more."

"A belief is thought that over time gains strength because a lot of other thoughts are attached that support this idea, and that can happen very quickly. And because it's so strong you think it's true—the truth. But that doesn't mean that it stops being a thought. It's just a thought that people made up."

"I didn't make this up! There are hundreds of people who have this belief."

"Just because many people have same belief doesn't make it the truth. You know better than that."

"Shut up! Okay? That's it! We're done. We're done!"

They sat in silence again. Many moments passed.

Jose again broke the silence. "You mean like the earth was flat?"

"Yes!" Gabriela said. "Just like that! There was a certain moment in time when people thought this was truth, and rules were created around it, and maps were drawn, and everybody followed it as if it was a fact. And it wasn't."

Jose tried to grasp something. "I guess a belief is the truth until proven wrong."

Jose was a multigenerational gang member. This was his world. The discussion disoriented him. "I don't want to talk about this any more," he growled.

Another kid said, "Well, she doesn't mean what she's saying," and offered some other explanation to try to soften the blow.

Gabriela said, "No, that's not what I mean. What I said is what I meant."

Jose said, "It's time to go anyways. See you."

Gabriela worried about him. Jose seemed disoriented. Maybe next week she'd suggest they have a one-on-one session together. But the next week he seemed fine, back to a nice feeling. He said he talked to

85

his girlfriend about turning herself in to the police, because her baby needed parents, so she needed to go ahead and get it over with now so she'd be able to be there for the kid when he got older and needed common sense and wisdom.

Jose was about to spend three years in a permanent placement. On his last day he asked Gabriela if she would be willing to have dinner with the guys.

She said, "I would love to."

Before they stared to eat Jose said, "We're going to pray. Would anybody like to start?"

Nobody did, so Jose took it on. "I ask God for wisdom," he said, "so I can finish my sentence and have strength for me and for everyone at this table." Jose prayed for everybody's families and girlfriends.

They began to eat. In the middle of the lighthearted, fun atmosphere, in the middle of the meal Jose leaned over to Gabriela: "You know," he said, "I was going to fight that first time I went to your class."

"I kind of thought you would," said Gabriela. "I'm just glad you didn't and listened to your wisdom."

"I had to act that way then," he said.

Gabriela nodded. At least that was his belief. It looked so real he had no choice. At the time he could see no other way.

That was the last time Gabriela ever saw him. Because he was in the juvenile system, once they left Juvenile Hall the trainers were required never to contact the kids again. But she still thinks of him often. He taught her that anyone can change. Because of how she saw him initially she had almost written him off and called the guards. But he changed—a jaw-dropping physical transformation in front of Gabriela's very eyes.

Or had he changed, really? Which was the real Jose? He had looked so mean, and so much older at first. When he started smiling he was a beautiful kid with dimples, and Gabriela almost missed it.

But she didn't.

What we see is what we get, and then we act out of what we get, which we made up in the first place.

VIII. In Low Levels of Consciousness It Is Unwise to Believe, Trust or Follow Our Thinking

Two girls about nine and eleven years-old splashed around happily in a swimming pool when I arrived to swim laps. I figured I'd give them three-quarters of the pool and I would swim in the other quarter close to the far wall.

After about ten laps I felt something bump against me. Since no sharks were in sight it had to be one of the girls. "Sorry," I said, and kept swimming.

A few minutes later I got knocked into again. Then again. Then again. The girls kept crashing into me. I began to feel a little annoyed. I had kindly given them most of the pool, and they had to stray into my end?! I usually swim for a half-hour and during that half-hour I don't like to be interfered with. It's a meditative time for me. I was about to say something out of my annoyance when I remembered what business I was in.

Still swimming, the thought popped into my head, "What is making me feel bothered right now?" I went into reflection.

I realized the reason I felt mild irritation was because I thought they were in my way and inconsiderate. "They have three-quarters of the pool, and they can't even stay in their own area!"

This interested me. The only reason I felt annoyed was because of my thinking that they were being inconsiderate. But "inconsiderate" existed in my own head! I realized I didn't know if they were being inconsiderate or not. I had no idea what was on their minds. Meanwhile, still swimming, I got bumped into again.

I thought, "Maybe they're really careless; maybe they just have no regard for others." I could easily see where that thought, believed,

Jack Pransky

would lead to anger. Anger is more serious than annoyance—some level farther away from our Health and wisdom.

The vertical continuum suddenly popped into my head. Near the bottom I'd be furious. To be furious I'd have to have a thought something like, "They're bumping into me on purpose. They're out to get me." Yup, if I had that thought and really believed it I would be furious. Some percentage of people do get furious in situations like this, and out of that fury, they lash out.

I had just traveled down the ladder:

↓ Mildly irritated & annoyed -- because they're inconsiderate
↓ Angry   -- because they're really careless
↓ Furious   -- because they're purposely doing it
                                 to me

If I went down the ladder, could I not also go up? I realized I would feel nothing—neutral—*if* I thought they were simply oblivious and had no idea what they were doing. Neutral is not a negative feeling; I am not bothered. This was an interesting possibility to me, because it seemed plausible. I now expected to be bumped into by oblivious children lost in play.

I then had the thought, "I wonder what would make them be oblivious in a situation like this, not notice I was there?" Suddenly I became interested in what made them tick. My feeling became a state of curiosity. I had jumped up another notch "above the line" of Health.

I then had another thought, "Maybe they don't even realize they're doing it," immediately followed by another: "Oops, I've bumped into people before without realizing it." I began to feel a little sheepish. I felt some humility.

Rising higher, another thought popped in: "Maybe their parents never taught them to be aware of their surroundings or watch out for others. Worse, what if their parents treat them as if they don't exist?" A feeling of compassion flooded over me with my next stroke.

"Ha!" I thought. "I don't know that, either! I could make up anything." I smiled under water. Suddenly I saw how amusing it is that we go around making all this up, and then we get a "real" feeling from whatever we've made up. How funny is that! It's like we're in our own little sit-com (when it's really a reality show).

Finally, I was hit with a feeling of gratefulness. "Wow," I thought, "If these kids had not bumped into me I would not have had this vivid experience of *seeing* these levels of consciousness in action." I truly did feel grateful. Thanks, kids.

Now I had jumped many rungs up the ladder above the line of Health and well-being. Most of us, given a choice, would like to live "above the line," and often the motives we attribute to others are the only thing that keeps us below it. I had just traveled up the ladder.

[Read from the bottom up:]

↑ Gratefulness	-- because this made me fully see this spectrum in action
↑ Humor	-- because we experience whatever motive we make up
↑ Compassion	-- because their parents may treat them as if they don't exist
↑ Humility	-- because I've bumped into others without realizing it
↑ A state of curiosity	-- because I'm interested in what makes them tick
↑ Neutral	-- because they're oblivious

- -

Maybe that is what is meant by "We are climbing Jacob's Ladder." Rising in levels of consciousness. Getting closer to the light, to the Source of our Health and well-being.

Don't forget, all these possibilities (and many more) existed at the time I had my first thought of annoyance; initially I didn't see the options. This is the way it is all the time, no matter in what circumstance we find ourselves. Fact: I was still swimming and being bumped into. Nothing about the situation had changed—except my own experience, which *I was making up by attributing motive.*

I know some people will say, "This is ridiculous! All you had to do was tell her [or ask her nicely] to move." Of course I could have done that, but that's not the point. I could have told her to move or quit bumping me and still been annoyed for the entire rest of my swim. I'm talking about my own experience of life here; what I get to live with. As it turned out, as I reflected on all this I had an increasingly better experience while swimming.

Mostly, in any given moment, we see what is right in front of us, as if looking down a tunnel or through a pair of binoculars. We don't realize a vertical dimension also exists—a continuum of levels of consciousness, from connection with our pure spirit within to the darkest suicidal or horribly violent thoughts. In every new moment the potential exists always for us to be at higher (or lower) levels. If that isn't hopeful I don't know what is.

We are always going up and down, down and up. Wherever we go there is always more to see within any situation or circumstance or when confronted by any person.

The two easiest ways I know of to drop levels is being hit with a low state of mind or being overtaken by a habit of thinking.

* * *

As I walk from "P" Street onto Nantasket Beach near Boston sometimes the beach is so packed with a blanket of rocks I think the sand is gone forever. A month later I walk onto the same beach and most of the rocks have cleared out, the sand smooth and pristine.

When walking onto a beach we don't realize we are walking onto constant change. All we see is one fixed point in time. In that moment we can only relate to what we see before us—unless we realize what is happening.

Sometimes we feel as if we're buried under a blanket of rocks—boulders even—the weight so debilitating we cannot imagine being free. Other times we don't. We don't realize we are in constant change. All we can relate to is that one point in time—unless we realize what is happening.

As waves of various sizes and strengths send rocks of various sizes and shapes onto the beach, so our thoughts bring emotions of various sizes and shapes to us depending on the quality of our thoughts. The waves giveth; the waves taketh away. Our thoughts giveth; our thoughts taketh away.

The beach has no control over the rocks it gets. The beach has no control of the waves breaking on its shore. The beach can only wait for different types of waves to come in and move the rocks, which they will do eventually because they've been doing it for millions of years. We have little control over most thoughts that pop into our heads; they simply show up. One day we wake up and our mind is covered by a blanket of heavy rocks, courtesy of our thoughts. The beach does not know how to stop the waves; we don't know how to stop our thoughts.

What is the key to living a rock-free life?

We can't! Rock n' roll is here to stay. The same is true with our mind-rocks. We are guaranteed sometimes to have thoughts that make us feel bad. We will always have moods. Human beings have different states of mind; that's simply the way it is.

However, we can realize our thought-moods don't mean anything. They're just passing through like the rocks coming in and moving out. If we let them pass on their own, they will. When they do our own pristine-ness again appears.

One day we see our partner as the greatest thing that ever happened to us. Another day we wish we'd never met.

One day we see a beautiful, intelligent human being. Another day the same person seems unattractive or stupid.

One day we see our house as warm and cozy and we're so happy to live there. Another day we see all its flaws and the work involved and wish we could move.

One moment we see our kids as little angels, so adorable and endearing and we are so grateful to have them; the next moment we see our kids as little monsters put on this earth to torment us and we wish we'd never had them.

One day we think we're good-looking. The next day we think we're ugly.

What could possibly cause this phenomenon?

Moods. Different states of mind.

In different states our thinking is different; with different thinking we have different moods. They are two sides of the same coin. Any difference in mood-thinking makes everything look different, even our looks.

Could it be that simple?

Yes! A low state of mind equals thinking at low levels of consciousness. The same thing is guaranteed to look worse at low levels than it does at higher levels. Which is real?

In a restaurant my daughter, Jaime, then age 23, nibbled lightly on the skin of a Habanero chili pepper. She mistakenly bit too deeply, hit the seeds, and her mouth began to burn so badly tears came to her eyes. She began to panic. In desperation her mouth cried out for water. She had to have water NOW! It drove her mad. But she also knew about Habanero peppers. She knew if she drank water it would make her mouth burn worse. As much as she desperately wanted to she could not afford to drink water. As hard as it was to resist, because she understood this phenomenon she resisted her temptation to pour every pitcher of water in the restaurant down her throat. Thus, she spared herself compounded agony.

The lower the mood the more real it looks and the more compelled we feel to take action. In low moods we are just dying to act, dying to yell at someone, dying to throw our computer across the room. But if we understand acting this way will make things worse, no matter how desperate or compelled we feel in that moment we will resist the temptation to go there, just as Jaime's understanding helped her resist the compelling temptation to drink water.

If we don't know about Habanero peppers, eat one, burn our mouth to bits and then drink water we will probably do it only once. We will learn from this very painful experience. Given how we often act in low moods, some people don't seem to learn so easily and keep repeating the same patterns.

As a private consultant I work for myself. I love my job. A downside is I don't like to hustle consulting jobs to make a living, so probably to my detriment I don't. Fortunately enough jobs have come in through word of mouth and my books, counseling and coaching to keep me afloat. Every once in a while if jobs are not coming in I experience fearful thoughts and think I have to hustle. But since that's not my style I'll think, "I can't believe I have to do this!" Then my entire worklife looks horrible. I've had thoughts I should give up training and consulting because there's no security in it, and I should go get "a real job."

I have a habit of thinking about marketing myself that does not serve me well, but it only bothers me when I'm in low spirits. Fortunately I realize this. If I gave up consulting while in a bad mood—if I made that decision then—I would be out of my own job, which at every other time I love. If I wait out the mood soon my work again looks perfect. I can't possibly have a better job (except that my boss is a real slave driver). I know I'm good at what I do because people change around me; they get better—not everyone, but more than enough to show me I'm on target and have played some small role in helping their lives improve. What could be better work than that! I couldn't be more thrilled and exhilarated than at the prospect of helping to improve another's life. The only time I don't love my work is when I'm in a low state. If I acted out of that, later I would regret it.

Let's say I'm trying to help a client, and it doesn't go so well. If I'm in a low mood I'll think, "Oh I'm not having any effect on people. Maybe I'm not good enough at this." Later my mood rises, and I'll think, "Gee, I couldn't help this person. I wonder what I missed so I can do better next time." Or I'll realize, "Well, he actually did change a little; he's not in as bad a state as he was when he walked in here." Or the thought might cross my mind that I have helped other people's lives change dramatically. My "reality" of my effectiveness depends on my state of mind in the moment, and my state of mind depends on whatever I happen to be thinking in that moment.

Do I really want to take action or make decisions out of low states? Do I really want to talk to my colleagues or my partner or my kids while in low states? I'm safe so long as I realize low-mood thinking is not "the way it is" and it will change eventually—so I wait it out before I make a move.

What if we were extremely depressed, saw life as utterly hopeless and had thoughts of suicide? If we don't understand the relationship between thinking, states of mind and our experience we could take the

93

suicidal thoughts seriously. It would be pretty terrible to follow suicidal thoughts then realize too late, "Oops, I see it differently now." Too bad! Not only suicide; many people get beaten or shot or raped or robbed because the perpetrator acts on thinking that he sees as real instead of realizing, "It's only the way it happens to look to me now, and if I wait out this feeling it will look differently later," If a change in seeing could happen with the extreme of suicide we certainly have the power to see the same in all aspects of everyday life.

Both Karla and Joan were depressed. Everything was going wrong. All they wanted to do was lie in bed under the covers and feel sorry for themselves. Karla would drag herself out of bed to take care of her business, feel okay, come back home, remember she was depressed, think there was something wrong with her and go back to bed. Joan, on the other hand, had something in the back of her mind that told her, "I know this will pass eventually, even if I can't seem to do anything about it right now. I know it doesn't really mean anything." This thought made the depression loosen its grip a bit, but she still couldn't shake it. The next morning she woke up and felt good. Everything looked better, though nothing had changed about her situation. She forgot her temporary depression.

What's the difference between Karla and Joan?

Karla believed the way she felt in a low state of mind was who she really was; she believed something was wrong with her. Joan knew it was only low-mood thinking, which happens to everyone from time to time, and it didn't mean anything about who she was. Karla saw her good moods as temporary relief from the way she was. Joan saw her bad moods as a temporary detour from her Health and well-being, which is who she *really* was.

The only difference is how they saw themselves in relation to their states of mind.

I stopped to park for two minutes to run into the post office. For only two minutes I ignored the parking meter. I came out to find a meter maid about to slap a ticket on my windshield.

"Wait!" I pleaded.

But she was in a low mood and wouldn't take it back.

Suddenly I let my own mood drop. But did I want to scream and yell at her? Did I want to storm over to the police station in outrage? Did I want to listen to the thinking telling me, "I'm never going to pay this unjust ticket!"? Or did I want to wait until I cooled down and my mood lifted and my thinking shifted, to see what my wisdom told me to do?

When my state of mind rose to better heights I thought, "Yeah, she may have been mean but, after all, I was the one who made the decision not to take a moment to put a quarter in the meter for even two minutes. Okay, so a quarter is cheaper than ten bucks. But in the grand scheme of things is even ten dollars really that big a deal? I'll know better next time." I've been much more careful with parking meters ever since.

If we follow our thinking in really low states we could quit our jobs, beat our kids, dump our friends, kick our dogs, put our fists through walls (or worse), torch our cars, get drunk, get depressed, give up on life, all of which we would regret later because we would have to pick up the pieces. Like Jaime with the Habanero chili pepper, we know that if we drink from that cup nothing good will come from our actions. Things will only get worse. So we bite our tongues and say nothing—take no action despite our compelling desire to attack. Before long we realize this feeling has passed. The situation looks a little clearer. Soon we wonder why we were so upset in the first place. Our wisdom kicks in. Then we can speak. When our state of mind changes it all looks different. It's an amazing thing.

We don't have to believe it when life looks hopeless, when it looks like our partner is a total jerk, when it looks like the world is out to get us, when it looks like we never should have had kids. We don't have to believe it because we know our self-created "reality" is a temporary illusion not to be acted upon. Our low-level consciousness is simply making it look as if it is reality. That's all! It means nothing. It's only a change in the quality of our thinking passing through in the grand scheme of life.

Most fights in this world occur because people take low-state-of-mind thinking seriously and feel compelled to act. The only problem is *trusting* that thinking when we feel that way and *following* it. The higher the mood, the higher the level of consciousness, and the more solutions and possibilities reveal themselves.

Of course things will look bad when we're in a bad mood. Expect it.

Can we be in a low state and still be in our Health? Yes! We can have all the angry, depressing, worried, anxious or bothered thoughts we want, so long as we know they mean nothing. Knowing our thinking will change when our mood rises, the situation will look different eventually, is a healthy thought even if we may not be able to pull ourselves out of it at the time. Sometimes we just feel like wallowing in self-pity for a while. That will do no harm if we know it really doesn't mean anything and will pass. Thus, we remain in our Health.

"All this is easy for you to say," some say. "I really have serious problems!"

I agree completely that the problems look and feel very real and serious. But the key word is "look." In a prolonged low state this thinking can last so long it can change our body chemistry [see Chapters I and VI].* And if chemicals change enough clinical depression can result, causing more depressed thinking.

It can also work the other way around. This explains why Lisa [Chapters I and VI], on depression medication for twelve years, was able to get off. Her thinking changed in huge ways with major insights. She realized the way she was thinking about herself, her daughter, her lot in life, wasn't *reality* and it didn't have to rule her. She realized this low thinking state may last a while, but it would change. This is what I meant earlier by our relationship to our thinking. She suddenly saw a different Lisa. Seeing this so deeply, without trying her body chemistry changed. She told her psychiatrist she no longer needed the medication. Her psychiatrist was baffled but admitted, whatever had happened, Lisa's body did not need the medication anymore. At a deep enough level, a change in Thought can change body chemistry.

---

* I realize other things also change body chemistry.

I am not saying people can go out of their way to think themselves out of depression. I am saying if a clinically depressed person has an insight of enough magnitude his or her body chemistry can change, and if this happens that person will no longer be clinically depressed. This is possible. I have seen it with my own eyes.

What about how we deal with other people when they're in low states? Suppose my partner says something nasty to me. Do I want to take it personally? Do I want to take it to heart?

Why would I want to take personally my partner's thinking in her low states? It's only her mood talking. Why should that have anything to do with me? I don't want her to take to heart the things I say when I am in a low mood; it would be nice if I allowed her the same leeway.

What if she really means it?

Most likely she doesn't. How do I know? Because if I say something nasty out of a low mood I don't really mean it. It's just how things look in that passing moment.

Some people seem to have a lot of those moments.

Does that mean we have to simply take whatever someone dishes out when they're in a low mood, no matter how horrible it is? No! If it's important enough we deal with it—later, when we both calm down and our wisdom kicks in. What's the rush? In a low mood it always looks as if there's a rush, but then even the urgency seems to pass.

The lower the mood, the easier it is to forget what we're seeing is illusion.

*   *   *

The other easy way to drop levels of consciousness is when a habit of thinking kicks in. A habit is a repetitive behavior driven by repetitive thoughts we believe and take seriously. Sometimes this thinking is so powerful it can create neural pathways in our brains through which subsequent thinking easily travels like a wheel in a rut.

Most people recognize smoking, drinking, being hooked on drugs, sexual promiscuity, eating and purging, etc., as habits. The field of addictions generally frowns upon calling smoking, drinking and drugging "habits." Personally, I think this is a mistake. A series of repetitive thoughts lies behind the development of every addiction and holds the addiction in place. If we look closely we can see so many people have kicked their physical addictions only to find themselves back doing it again. Why? Is it because it's a disease and they're at the mercy of that disease? I can see where the physical addiction could be called a disease, but a disease of thinking? My own logic tells me this doesn't make sense. Once the physical addiction has been kicked it seems to me people relapse because their thinking habits have not changed. In my view, not to call it a thinking habit does a disservice to people with addictions. Habitual thinking, seen for what it is, can be overcome; a disease that in our own minds lasts forever (and can only be kept at bay) can keep people feeling stuck in the addiction.

People don't realize many other things are also habits. People don't realize worry is a habit. I'm not talking about an isolated worry-thought about an isolated event; I'm talking about seeing everything through the eyes of worry. People don't realize lashing out in anger is a habit—again not an isolated burst, but when it becomes their typical way of responding. People don't realize judgment of others is a habit. People don't realize guilt is a habit (although people are more likely to admit guilt—and blame it on their religion or culture—than most other habits).

Behind every set of repetitive thoughts is a core belief that is its driving force. The dandelion metaphor (Chapter I) is an example. We pick up many of these beliefs from the way we were taught or treated when growing up. These core beliefs are illusions. Our folks made them up. We took them on. They probably picked them up from their folks. We may adjust them a little over time but they're insidious. They work on us mostly without our knowing it.

Behind each habit is also a thought of fear—fear of what would happen if we gave up the habit. Such thoughts hold the habit in place and make it difficult to break. Yet fear, too, is an illusion. We've made up what we're fearful of! Unless this fear is seen for the illusion it is it will not let go.

Consider people who have the habit of lashing out in anger if something doesn't go their way. Why would they do this? Some other thinking—a core belief—lies behind it, such as, "No one gets in my way!" A person seeing life through this belief will tend to lash out if someone gets in his way. Behind that may be another thought—a thought of fear, perhaps fear of losing control. Behind that there may be another thought that makes people think they need control. It's all very complex.

But does it make sense to try to unravel all this complex, hidden thinking, when it is so much easier to simply transcend it by seeing it all for the illusion it is?

Many people have a habit of smoking they would love to be rid of.* What is the core belief that drives someone to smoke in the face of indisputable evidence that it is horrible for their health?" For many it's, "It makes me feel good," or "I can quit whenever I want," or "Cancer or heart disease won't happen to me" or "It helps me calm down" or "It gives me an excuse to take a break and I wouldn't otherwise," and more. Likely behind that thinking is fear, possibly "I don't know how I'd be if I didn't smoke; I wouldn't feel right. What would I do? I'm not sure I'd make it through the day." If that thought were not recognized for what it is and transcended (as opposed to "worked on"), it would be mighty difficult for that person to quit smoking, even without the physical addiction.

Many people have eating habits, such as eating too much and feeling bad about themselves, or eating too much, purging and feeling bad about themselves. For some, the belief might be, "Everything in this society tells me I should be thin, therefore I shouldn't eat much— but I really want this piece of chocolate cake. I can't help myself! Maybe it won't cause too much harm. If I eat it I'll feel satisfied. It's so much easier just to do it." For some, the fear behind that might be, "Everything in my life feels out of control; if I eat whatever I want I have some control" or behind that may be: "I'm not okay as I am."

Don't forget, we are usually not aware we have these beliefs and fears, and when we're not aware of them we can't do anything about them. Again I'm not suggesting we look for them, mostly because that

---

* Again, I know the tobacco addictions field especially frowns upon the use of the word "habit" when it comes to smoking, but that may be because the field currently does not understand the primary role of Thought.

search is hard and can bring us down. Again it's better to see the illusion. If we do have a desire to see our own thinking habits—which I admit can be helpful at times—we would be wise to open ourselves to seeing something new about our habits, then get quiet, take it off our minds and see what comes.

Margaret was the oldest daughter of twelve children. When she became a pre-teenager she was expected to do all the cooking and cleaning and take care of the younger children. So she became a tremendous cook, cleaner and "caregiver." While she loved her parents dearly she always felt she needed their approval, so she also grew up feeling she had to continually prove herself. This especially reared its head whenever she met someone new.

This type of thinking becomes the lens through which we see life. This invisible lens drives us. Everything we see is filtered through this lens, as if we are always wearing a pair of strangely colored sunglasses (like yellow) that begin to look normal when we leave them on a while. This lens, through which we see life, is the main culprit. But we don't see it.

Some people believe that when something happens "out there" it causes them to act in certain ways. For example, if a kid gets "dissed" (disrespected), it means he has to slug or cut or shoot the kid who "dissed" him. A sexual offender sees someone attractive to him and he's got to go after her. A shoplifter sees something in a store and she's got to have it. The rest of us know this isn't true; the person in question does not. It's so real to her she thinks she has no choice but to act on it. It is easier to see this in others than in ourselves.

When something happens "out there" many of us believe it causes us to *feel* certain ways. Stress is a case in point. We think because we have too much to do in too little time it causes stress. We think the situation makes us stressed out. So long as we think that we're stuck with the stress. This feels just as "real" for us as it does for the person who goes after the kid or commits a crime.

The feeling is so compelling it drives us to act the way we do.

This feeling comes from what we think about it. Cognitive psychologists understand this. But many cognitive psychologists also believe what happens out there is reality, but we can think about that reality in many different ways, and people can change the way they think about that reality. For example: "Given the fact that this person insulted me, I can think differently about it." This is where positive thinking or reframing comes in.

None of this takes into account *the way we see it* in the first place; that no matter what happens out there we are seeing it through a *thought-lens* that shapes and drives our thoughts. The way we see it comes from thinking we don't know we're thinking that is hidden in

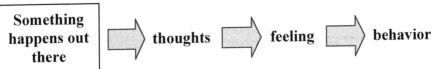

our lens. This lens contains numerous beliefs: how we see ourselves; what we think is right and wrong; what causes us to see right and wrong as we do; how we see the event; how we interpret the event in light of how we see right and wrong—and so much more. Our lens determines the "reality" we see. This lens lies behind why we think, feel and act the way we do. Our lens is the culprit.

Back to the example: If someone speaks to us in a way some would find insulting, feeling insulted is not a given, no matter what words were used. I may not see what they said as an insult in the first place. If I saw the guy as mentally ill, for example, I wouldn't feel insulted given the same words; I would attribute his words to his

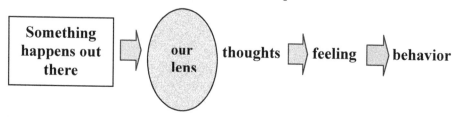

illness—it's got nothing to do with me. If I saw the guy as well-meaning and doing his best but lost, I wouldn't feel insulted; I might feel bad for him for living in such an unhappy world. I'm not going out of my way to think such things; they're what my lens is telling me to see, but I don't often know it.   We'd be surprised to know what is

lurking in our lens.

Imagine this lens as a cookie. The cookie is already baked. Suppose it came out burnt. We could try to make that burnt cookie taste better but it's tough to make a burnt cookie taste good—it's too late. Yet the cookie had to be baked someplace. It came from a *creative process* in the kitchen. The lens may be the culprit—it's what's behind our feeling bad—but the answer is not in the lens. The creative process is where our answers lie. The answer to a better tasting cookie is not in the cookie; the answer is in the kitchen. The kitchen could bake another, better tasting cookie[*]. Our creative process can create a different lens. Mind, Thought and Consciousness are our creative powers. We have inadvertently used these creative powers to make up the thought-lens we see through, out of which we then think, feel and act. Trying to unravel the lens is like trying to make a burnt cookie taste better. Our power is to realize what is in our lens is an illusion created from our use of Mind, Consciousness and Thought, and to know another lens might be created or no lens might be created. Another "reality" is automatically created as soon as we realize *we are the kitchen.*

---

[*] I first heard this metaphor from Keith Blevens—thank you, Keith—and he may have heard it from someone else; then one day I truly *saw* it for myself.

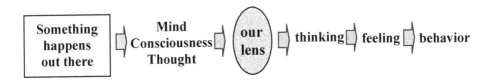

Imagine what we miss when our focus is on changing one's behavior, or delving deeply into one's feelings (that we've only made up by how we see the situation or person), or striving to reframe one's thoughts. Imagine how spirits could get lowered or how people could get lost when trying to unravel or muck around in the lens without realizing its source, where it really comes from, the source from which it is all created.

Imagine the power if a prospective murderer, rapist, robber, abuser or addict understood the way thought worked and said to himself, "Even though I feel so compelled to do this right now and want to so badly, I know it's only my thinking talking—I've made up this feeling, it's not reality and I don't have to believe it or go after it."

Crista's Story

A few people have bad reactions when they hear about TheThree Principles for the first time, perhaps for some because it is foreign to anything they've heard before, perhaps because they don't want the responsibility, perhaps because it sounds too simple, perhaps other reasons. Crista's reaction was among the worst I had ever experienced. During the first day of training she seemed downright hostile. She did seem to mellow a bit during the second day, but she didn't say much to me. I didn't see her again for two years when, to my surprise, she signed up for a Health Realization II course at Woodbury College*. When she arrived I could not believe the change in her. She became one of the most enthusiastic students I ever had.

Throughout my life I have experienced the many negative effects of my own unhealthy thoughts and decisions. For many years I struggled as I continued to travel down what seemed to be dead-end roads and one-way streets. There have been countless events resulting in self-destructive behaviors. For many years I struggled with self-esteem and worth. I battled many internal frustrations, resulting in personal isolation from close friends and family members. As I continued to live these everyday conflicts, I was able to find comfort with alcohol. Then I had a battle with alcoholism. Oftentimes the only face I would see as I gazed the mirror was that of despair.

After seeing my dismal face stare me down, I realized that my efforts to live my life were not of a healthy person. Suddenly I realized that I was living life to please everyone else. It resulted in increased frustrations and unhappiness. Day after day I lived often feeling trapped, like there was no way out.

Roughly two years ago I recognized these unhealthy behaviors. I was feeling as though my life held no significant meaning and no purpose. The only happiness I knew were the joys of being a mother, which at times were extremely challenging. After exploring many relationships, which ended in what appeared to be failure (due to my unhealthiness), I knew the time had finally come for drastic changes. So, after careful consideration and many sleepless nights, I decided to return to school. Somewhere there was a voice, which kept me up at night, providing me with very clear and direct life instructions. Little did I know that this voice I was hearing was the voice of my very own wisdom.

Somewhere in my decision to return to school and experience situations with positive outcomes, I began recognizing the importance of pleasing myself and being happy. I did not know how I was going to accomplish this. Those who I cared about most were telling me that I was never going to succeed, that I did not have what it took to reach this goal. I received this resistance from all my close friends and family members. This fueled my efforts toward personal success.

Entering Woodbury College as an adult student, I faced an increasing number of challenges, not only internal but external. I was introduced to Health Realization through a prevention workshop. Here I was, sitting in an atrium filled with other adult students, listening to Jack talk about mind, the power of thought and our ability to be conscious. As I sat through this workshop I could not help but think that this was just another gimmick, another brain-washing tactic to get us to buy into Jack's perspective on health. As I listened to Jack "carry on" about the three principles, I was anticipating a catch. Throughout the rest of the day Jack continued to talk about the three principles, the many accounts of success, about the innate health and wisdom we all have, and ways in which we all can operate from this place of tranquility and peacefulness. As Jack was explaining this to the group, I could not help think, " Oh yeah, sure Jack, if this were true, then we would all be walking around happy, free from worry, sadness, depression and fear. Most importantly, Jack, we would definitely have no need to be sitting here listening to you sell this information to us."

Oddly enough, through my resistance, something Jack said sparked curiosity. As I was driving home from the class

I could not help but listen to his words. Though I tried to ignore his voice, I was unsuccessful. Jack stated that we create our thoughts, therefore they can change, and with patience we all would be able to hear that tiny voice in the back of our minds guiding us in one direction or another. Jack referred to this as listening to our inner wisdom. I had another sleepless night. I could not help but wonder about the validity of Jack's words. I had yet another day of this workshop, so I decided to test this material out for myself. Driving in, I could not help but think of the endless possibilities that could be in my future. So with this increased level of curiosity, I entered the second day with a new attitude and an increased level of consciousness. By the end of the day I was beginning to feel something I had not felt in a very long time. Suddenly I was feeling a sense of freedom, a sense of responsibility, a sense of happiness. Unexpectedly, I was beginning to vision my once perceived dead-end roads as roads under construction. My choices were like the yellow traffic light. For the first time I felt I could go forward with my healthy decisions, and do so with healthy caution.

Why was Health Realization introduced to me at this point in my life? I am not really sure. However, I do know that it was a true gift, almost in preparation for what my future held in store. Unexpectedly, a few months after taking part in Jack's workshop and continuing to read and research Health Realization, my youngest daughter contracted a viral illness, which threatened her life. Hannahlei was 15-months old at the time. She was walking, talking and full of energy. She had the most beautiful blonde hair and baby blue eyes you could ever imagine. Her personality was infectious to all she came in contact with. Her smile could melt any hardened heart. Instantly, without any warning, her life was swept from under her, without any explanation of why or how. This viral illness left Hannahlei unable to walk, talk, sit, stand, even hold her own head up. Her hands and feet so contracted that she was unable to open her fingers or spread her tiny toes. As each day passed, her condition worsened. Doctors, nurses, medical teams and specialists were unable to diagnose or treat her condition. The only thing we were able to see was the constant regression of her physical health. What was I to do? My hands were tied. All I could do was hold my precious child in my arms, staring at her chest as it caved in and out, grasping for the very breath keeping her alive. Constant thoughts were running through my head about life without her. All I could think was that I was going to lose her for good.

Suddenly it hit me like a ton of bricks: Health Realization! Instantly I had a ray of hope. Within seconds my negative thoughts and fears about Hannahlei's illness transformed into positive ones. I began cherishing each and every moment in a way that gave me strength and courage to face this illness alongside her, but with a newly found hope. Though Hannahlei's physical health was not improving, my inner health was. Hannahlei continued her radiant smile, even in the face of her despair. We began to find humor in things that once were not so funny.

As the days passed I was able to look at this devastating situation as a gift. Here was my child suffering, and it brought our family closer together. For months on end my two children and I walked a very fine line, able to face this crisis in a way that allowed us to remain healthy, despite all the physical complications and impairments. Days that once seemed as though my life was crumbling down in front of my very own eyes suddenly were days of building up strength, determination, health and will.

Today, Hannahlei has surpassed all clinical prognoses of her life span. She is close to a full recovery in relation to the white matter in her brain that was destroyed, with comparatively minimal physical impairments and challenges. A lot has since rejuvenated, unknown to medical knowledge. Otherwise, she has a very long ways to go. She has been left with long-term, even life-long delay and impairments.

Though medicine was helpful in treating her "undiagnosable" condition, I believe being connected with inner health not only contributed to saving Hannahlei's life but is also the responsible factor in maintaining the balance we all needed to pull through this most difficult situation.

As a result of being exposed to Health Realization, I have been able to accept that the past is the past. I now recognize the importance of being in the now, and experiencing all that my thoughts have to offer. It's nice knowing that I hold the power to create my own destiny. I feel that I now am able to model health in a way that not only brings me to a deeper place of inner health and peace, but has assisted my family in modeling health in a very therapeutic way.

Hannahlei, now 3, and Lindsay, age 8, find strength and energy from their inner health. I believe that I have modeled health in a way my children have been able to mimic. Through we have very trying times, many of which would have once brought us deep down, we are now able to face these problems with a healthy perspective and newly found attitude. Health Realization has definitely made it possible for us to not only reconnect with our health, but also to remain healthy in these times of need.

IX. To Deeply Listen to Others Instead of to Our Own Thinking Gives Us A Richer Experience

The day after Gabriela and I finished conducting a three principles training in Puerto Rico, with everyone experiencing nice, warm feelings, we took a hike with some participants, most of whom knew each other. We hiked down a long, semi-steep trail to a small waterfall, where I slipped on a rock and nearly fell in. Some of us went swimming. Everyone had a good time. As we hiked back out and emerged from the rainforest we saw two men from our group who had walked ahead of us standing in the parking lot in a heated argument.

It escalated. It looked as if they might come to blows. It was the antithesis of everything we had talked about in the training. Apparently they had forgotten everything they'd learned, and it hadn't taken long.

I have no idea what possessed me, but impulsively I walked smack into the middle of the argument and stood between them. I could feel the heat from both sides.

"May I say something here?"

Surprised, they both stopped arguing for a moment. All eyes were upon me. Gabriela sat off to the side thinking, "What is he doing?"

I said, "You know, when two people have a disagreement, it is really helpful to take a step back from one's own position and listen very deeply to the other side until you can really understand that side. That way it's a lot easier to reach a meeting of the minds."

That is a true statement. I shouldn't have said it.

Why? Because I didn't take the time to listen to what they really needed to hear in that moment. Despite my talk about listening, my own listening was terrible.

It's not that it wouldn't have been helpful for them to do what I suggested. The point is, at that moment, both were far too riled up to listen to the other's point of view.

Why hadn't I listened well enough? Because once I walked into the middle of the argument I suddenly had the thought, "Uh oh, now what? What am I doing here?" I had visions of them going after each other with me in the middle. I felt a touch of insecurity—it probably didn't help that I had heard one of them had once settled a fight with a machete—and my mind started scrambling for what to do next.

It is difficult to listen when the mind is running scared.

Interestingly, one of them sort of heard what I suggested and tried to listen, but the other guy didn't hear me at all. He kept up his heated side of the argument under the guise of, "Okay, you listen to me!"

Their argument was over the fact that one of the men, a former massage therapist, gave a massage to the other's 14-year-old sister (on a massage table always set up in the middle of a living room full of people). Her older brother felt very uncomfortable about this. He asked the guy to stop and he didn't.

"I'm a professional and I would never take advantage of your sister," he said, heatedly. "It's an insult that you would think I would."

"But it made me uncomfortable, and I asked you to stop and you didn't!"

Back and forth and back and forth.

Keep in mind these guys were sort of friends and had just spent three days together in peace and harmony. Now there was none. They weren't listening and were about to come to blows.

If I'd had my wits about me I would have stepped back a bit and paused before jumping in. I would have cleared my head and deeply listened awhile before making a move. I would have asked myself, "What is needed here right now?" or "What do they need to hear right now?" and waited. If I had, I may have heard that they were much too hot to hear anything and needed simply to calm down. I may have heard that they were much too serious and needed to lighten up as the first order of business. Had I heard this at the time I still may still have walked into the middle of their anger but said something like, "Peace, my brothers." Possibly that may have stopped them in their tracks for at least a moment so they could regain their bearings and connect once again with what was important.

Instead, while what I said did not make matters worse, neither did it make things better. The argument remained unresolved, though we did manage to scoot them off into different cars and drive away, Gabriela with one; me with the other. What I said wasn't helpful because I hadn't listened well enough before leaping in.

In a Calvin and Hobbes cartoon Calvin's mother is in the living room reading a magazine. Calvin is at the doorway sticking his head in from outdoors. He yells to her from across the room, "Mom! Oh MOM!"

His mother says, "Calvin, how many times do I have to tell you not to yell across the room to me like that. If you've got something to say to me come over here and tell me."

Calvin looks puzzled, goes in, walks over to her across the carpet and says, "I stepped in dog doo. What should I do?"

This epitomizes the kind of listening we often do, especially with our children.

The main problem with our listening is our own thinking. When listening to others we don't realize that we often drift off into our own heads and lose the other person, who continues to blabber on as if we really are listening. Our thoughts leave the person we're supposed to be listening to! Why? Maybe what the person says reminds us of something about ourselves; maybe we clue into their eyes or what they're wearing; maybe we'll start to think about what we need to get at the store later, and so forth. Our consciousness follows our thinking wherever it travels. Therefore, we are no longer conscious of the other person. Our consciousness has jumped to whatever is going on in our own minds. We lose all connection.

When I realized this, any illusion I had that I was a good listener went right out the window. I realized I needed to listen at a different, deeper level. So I learned what I call "deep listening."[*] I tried it out and my listening ability skyrocketed. I began hearing way beyond people's words. For example, once someone said to me, "My son is nasty to me, even though I give him everything he wants. I don't know what to do." I heard, "Wow, she has a victim mentality and doesn't see how she's using her victim-thinking against herself."

How did I hear that? She didn't say it.

I don't know. I heard it deep within myself. But it's not as big a mystery as it seems.

When parents have little babies they are nearly all expert deep listeners. Babies have no words to tell us what they want at the moment, so we become experts at picking up cues or whatever it is that tells us what is on their minds. We come to know the meaning of different kinds of cries. We are totally present with them. We have a very close connection and can feel what they want from us—not all the time but much of the time. If the kid is happy we are completely fascinated with what s/he is trying to say. If the kid is sad or uncomfortable we are totally curious about what is going on because the baby has no words to describe it. What we do naturally with little babies who can't talk, or with pets to know what they want, is precisely what deep listening is.

Deep listening is being completely present with another human being with nothing extraneous on our minds. A close connection often results.

Deep listening is picking up a feeling. It is listening via intuition.

Deep listening is being fascinated with the other person and curious about what is on his or her mind.

Deep listening is listening to what people are really trying to say, instead of to their words.

The only way we can pick up what people are really trying to say behind their words is if our own minds are clear. When our own thinking is on our minds we're only listening to ourselves and not to

---

[*] Others call it "vertical listening," or in working with teenagers I've called it "extreme listening." I first really learned how to deep listen from Linda Pransky—thank you, Linda.

the other person. *Our own thinking interferes with deep listening*; in fact, it is the only thing that can.

This means, when someone is talking to us, if we had no thoughts we would automatically be deep listening. But it is impossible to have no thoughts. So we simply allow the thoughts to come in and pass through without following where they might take us. More on this later.

Unfortunately, as soon as our kids learn to talk we forget our natural talent for deep listening. Why? Because we start listening to their words, instead of being attuned to the other cues or what they're really trying to say. The words then become all we hear. We no longer listen to what's behind the words. We often lose that truly close connection. We forget we have this enormous capacity to pick up what people are feeling and what they are really trying to get at. Yet this natural ability to be fabulous listeners never leaves us—not just for our kids, for anyone. We only forget we have this incredible talent, and we stop using it.

I am not inclined to go into detail about how to *do* deep listening because there really is nothing to do. Deep listening is simple: It is the natural way we were meant to listen. If we weren't inadvertently interfering with our listening with our own thinking we would automatically be deep listening. Thus, it's more of a "not doing," a "relaxing into." If there's nothing to do, how can there be details?

Some readers may be wondering if we're not listening to the words then how can we be paying attention to what the person is saying? The irony is we're actually more attentive. We understand what they're saying but at a deeper level. This has nothing to do with watching body language, nor the "Active Listening" technique of repeating or reflecting back what the person is saying. All that stuff usually keeps our minds cluttered. Instead, with nothing on our minds, we want to simply *be present, be fascinated by or curious* about what that person is really trying to say, what that other person's world looks like, what would make that person see things this way? None of that has anything to do with their words. At the same time, we're still somehow

Jack Pransky

registering what they're saying; it's not like we're not hearing them at all.

Why am I spending time on deep listening to others when this book is about *self* help? Because deep listening is one of the keys that provides closeness and power in relationships.

Think of it: When a love relationship begins we are usually expert deep listeners. We are totally present with the other person. We feel incredible closeness. We are fascinated with what the other is saying. We are completely curious about the person. We don't care about the words so much; we are interested in the feeling. We put aside what is on our minds so we can drink in the other's spirit. Perfect deep listening!

Imagine being with our partners this way most of the time. Wouldn't our relationships be incredible? When do we lose this? Often we get distracted by what we think our partner should be like or what our partner should be doing—all thoughts—and we stop listening.

Imagine being fascinated by what someone—anyone—is really trying to say. We would automatically be great listeners. We would be automatically tuned into the person and would pick up a good feeling because interest or fascination simply feels good. The feeling we often pick up is a close connection with the humanity of the person.

Imagine what it would be like to be curious or completely interested in how another person sees his world. Imagine being able to listen until we actually understand what that person's world looks like to her, or why it makes sense to him to be doing whatever he's doing.

The more our partner or anyone feels we are interested in his or her view and feels a close connection, the more our partner will be inclined to relax, which calms the mind and perhaps even inspires new insights.

One day in a Health Realization training in Ohio I was talking about how we can experience any situation from different levels of understanding, and when we're seeing things negatively we have inadvertently made up seeing it that way. Suddenly a participant went into a tirade about how this just sounded like some other psychology and, besides, she didn't see how this could work with kids.

I said, "It has worked with kids. It does work with kids."

She shook her head emphatically. "I can't see how."

"Are you saying you don't believe it's true?" I asked, sincerely wanting to know what she meant.

I was about to give her some examples of where and how it has worked with kids but she said, "I'm not calling you a liar. I just can't see how." Then more negativity than I had heard in a long time spewed from her.

She hadn't heard one thing I said. I got an "uh oh" feeling. I could feel myself beginning to get a bit defensive (very rare for me in a training; I must have been in a low mood), and while she talked I could feel myself about to respond out of that defensiveness.

All of a sudden I fell into deep listening (which I admit I hadn't been doing up to that point), and an overwhelming feeling came over me.

I thought, "Wow, this woman lives in such a negative world!" I felt so bad for her. "She must be in such pain to think she has to live like this."

A wave of deep compassion flooded over me. As soon as I felt it my entire body relaxed. Now I saw this woman completely differently, and what she said no longer affected me. I then was able to respond in a way that took the sting out of what she said, and it elevated the mood of the entire group. Had I responded without first deep listening I may have had a problem on my hands.

When we meet someone at a meeting or at a party or over a dinner or anywhere, how do we enter a conversation with that person? Do we enter it to put forth what's on our minds, to put out what we know, or do we enter it to learn something new, to take in whatever we can from the other person? More often than not, it seems most people would rather talk than listen. We seem far more interested in expressing what we have to say than hearing what they have to say. The problem is, when we're either talking or thinking about what we want to say,

Jack Pransky

we're not listening. Why? Because we can't have an empty, receptive mind if our own thoughts are cluttering it.

Again, it is no mystery. Many of us naturally experience deep listening when out in nature taking in the multitude of sounds through our senses. Many of us naturally experience this when listening to music we love. We have already talked about our natural listening ability when we fall in love or are present with a baby or a pet. It is possible to listen to a stranger or any human being the same way. What a concept! We may not feel love, but we'll have a better experience. Listening to nature or to loved music often gives us a good feeling. This is the type of feeling we tend to pick up when deep listening to an interesting human being.

What if the person is not interesting, you say? What if they're boring? What if they're obnoxious? What if they're nasty?

Let's say we experience any of these. What goes on in our minds? Take "boring," for example. We might say to ourselves, "Oh God, this person is so boring! He says the same things over and over again and doesn't realize no one else has the slightest interest in what he's saying."

We must have a lot on our minds.

Hidden in the background of our minds (our lens) may be an idea of what "boring" means to us. If we've been with this person before we may have memories of him in action and how we felt at those times. Our minds might drift, or we may tune out altogether and imagine ourselves somewhere else. We may get irritated that we have to be stuck here listening to this boring person. All that is a lot to have on our minds! A downward spiral of thinking begins and we have an unpleasant experience. The further down the spiral goes the worse our experience gets. With all of that on our minds our listening plummets, because it is the opposite of an empty mind. The more we have on our minds the less we are able to listen, period.

Instead of experiencing "boring," suppose we became fascinated by what would make this person come across this way? What would make him think he was coming across well? What must his life be like? How does he see the world? Would that not be interesting? To listen for any of those would be to have a completely different

116

experience of the same person—likely a more pleasant experience. Does this person realize how he comes across? If not, why not? What does he see that makes him think this is the thing to do? Those would be interesting questions to listen for.

Some astute readers may be thinking, "I thought you said to have nothing on our minds. Aren't those questions having something on our minds?"

On the surface it looks that way, but we don't really want even those questions on our minds. This is another paradox. We don't want to be in a conversation with any of those questions or anything on our minds. Out of our own quiet mind when listening, questions like those or others may occur to us. We might ask the question of ourselves, such as, "I wonder what his world looks like," but then we want to immediately forget it and simply get quiet again. In this way we are setting our intention to pick up an answer to our question while still keeping a clear mind.

What do we have to lose? With all the other thinking we're doing, we're already having a lousy experience with the person we see as boring.

The irony is that we would naturally feel a close connection with other humans if we didn't have other extraneous thoughts. What we're trying to get we already have, and we can only interfere with it.

Another irony is that deep listening is for our own benefit. Sure, it feels good to the other person because everyone loves to be truly listened to, but by deep listening we get more goodies out of our time with other people. We get much more out of those moments. At stake is nothing less than our own enjoyment and satisfaction. It doesn't take any more time. Nor do we have to deep listen at all. We simply get an experience from whatever form of listening we do.

One day while driving I didn't feel like listening to music or to my own thoughts, so I turned on the radio and bumped into Dr. Joy Brown. She's famous for giving advice to people who call her program, and often it's based on common sense. Someone called and talked about a friend with whom she got into arguments about the same things over and over and it was affecting the relationship. The good doctor said something like, "If you have an argument with a friend about the same thing over and over again, such as politics, just agree that you're not going to talk about it."

That may be common sense but Dr. Joy did not demonstrate deep listening. I mean nothing against Joy Brown; I'm only suggesting advice is another way to keep people looking outside themselves for answers. It's like saying, "If you just listen to me (since you can't seem to listen to your own common sense), everything will be fine." Advice is only helpful if one has a new insight and thinking changes; otherwise advice will bump up against the other person's thought-lens.

Before giving advice if Dr. Joy Brown had deeply listened to the caller she may have heard what I heard: This caller was in pain because she felt she was losing a close connection with her friend because they saw two different worlds and she didn't know how to bridge the divide. "Just agree not to talk about those things" does not speak to this underlying issue.

If those two friends were taught how to deeply listen to each other they would gain a deeper appreciation of the other's world and would feel an even closer connection. Otherwise they're still going to have unresolved thinking hanging over their heads in their relationship. Deep listening gives people a deeper experience of each other without the emotion that arises from opposing positions.

If we disagree with someone, instead of coming up with arguments and feeling the tension, we could listen with curiosity for what makes sense to the other person. What would make this other person see things their way? What would make my partner—or my kids, or my business associates, or my neighbors, or the cashier who was nasty to me—see it that way? That's fascinating stuff, compared with arguing from our point of view and trying to push our "reality" onto someone else. We could ask questions of them to see it even better. We want to get to the point where we can truly say to ourselves, "Oh, I see why she sees it this way! I get it." This is listening behind the words.

This doesn't mean we have to agree; it only means we understand what makes them see it the way they do. This means we listen until it makes perfect sense to us why she is taking her position given the way she sees her world. If the other person is then willing to listen to us in the same way and hears why we see things the way we do, we maintain or develop a close bond, even though we may still disagree on a point we consider important. Even if they can't see it the way we do we're still in a much better position to have a meeting of the minds because we understand better what the other person needs from us. (Imagine if Democrats and Republicans, conservatives and liberals actually took the time to deeply listen to each other for the good of the country.)

A meeting of the minds is always better than a butting of the heads.

The alert reader will recognize this is what I was trying to convey to the two arguing guys at the beginning of this chapter. But at that time I wasn't listening well enough to hear what they needed in the moment because their minds (and mine) were anything but calm. If minds are calm, this approach to resolving conflicts through deep listening is especially helpful with our kids, spouses, people at work, neighbors, or anyone we might be having difficulty with. To be able to truly hear, "Oh, I see why they see it this way!" is to elevate our thinking—in fact, elevate both sides—about the situation.

Plus, the more we listen to others the more they will have a tendency to listen to us.

The next time we went to Puerto Rico I found that Julia's life [the psychologist from Chapter V] had improved measurably. She was no longer depressed. She was less stressed. She was more effective with her clients. Still her life had bumps. Though she worked very hard at her job many times she felt guilty she was not doing enough or was slacking off. As I deeply listened to her it occurred to me that she still saw a lot of "reality" (the way things are) in many aspects of her life, and if she saw more illusion (creations of her own thinking) she would reach an even deeper level of understanding.

One evening Julia decided she would extend her vacation for another day. After all, she'd been moving into a new apartment and still had to do a great deal to get it ready, and besides, Gabriela and I were visiting again. She then became riddled with guilt.

While taking a walk in the city Julia suddenly became famished and said she really needed to eat. By the time we actually sat down in a restaurant she had completely lost her appetite. Instead, she had a terrible stomachache.

Julia told me this happened often—every time she started to feel guilty about slacking off. While such pains used to be constant, now they came only every few days and would last only ten or fifteen minutes until she remembered it was only her thinking and she didn't have to take it so seriously. Yet, as she was saying this her eyes filled with tears.

"Because our feelings feel so real," I said softly, "what we're seeing really looks real to us. All your reasons for feeling guilty truly look real—that's the job of consciousness—but they're really only illusion. Inadvertently you're making up your own standards for your behavior, then making up whether you're meeting those standards, then making up how upset you should be because you aren't meeting your standards. If you truly saw all of that as illusion you would not be caught so much in that 'reality.'"

"Yes," said Julia, "when I'm counseling others I have told them this. I told them when I was really depressed and just lying at home feeling sorry for myself I decided I would go out dancing, and for those few hours I would forget that I was depressed. Then I would come back home and be feeling better in spite of myself. Then I would get depressed again, but during those few hours I would forget."

"Hmm. That's not quite what I'm saying."

"What do you mean?"

"I'm not talking about temporarily forgetting what one sees as 'real.' It's deeper than that." For some reason I was unable to articulate clearly enough what I meant.

"It *is* about forgetting," Julia argued, "and I *do* understand what you're saying."

Ironically, during this time she forgot her stomach pain and became hungry again.

"That's what I meant about forgetting what you see is 'reality,'" I said. "We're talking about 'forgetting' in different ways. I'm talking about what happened to you right now. All of a sudden the guilt you felt a moment ago became unimportant to you because you were engaged in an argument about forgetting. You forgot the reality of the guilt that caused the stomach pain, but you didn't go out of your way to forget it like you did when you went out to dance."

To Julia it was the same thing. She became a bit irritated.

As I listened to her something nagged at me. I said, "If you could really deeply see what I'm trying to say, you would be free."

She stopped in her tracks. Her face betrayed a look of fear. What was that?

We left the restaurant, walked back to her car and began to drive off. I was hearing something deep beyond my intellect but I couldn't put my finger on exactly what it was.

We passed by an overlook where the moon bounced light off the waves in the otherwise pitch-black ocean. We stopped to take in the beautiful sight.

We stood there in silence, gazing at the beauty.

In the silence I asked myself what Julia wasn't seeing. I knew the real issue wasn't what Julia was arguing about; it was something deeper. But what? It was like having something on the tip of my tongue, just out of reach. I became quiet again, emptied my mind and focused on the dark, moonlit ocean and stars.

Suddenly I saw it! I heard way beyond her words. Julia was afraid of freedom.

I told Julia what I saw. It deeply affected her. She knew it was true, though she'd never realized it before, at least not at that level. Somehow it was more comforting to have her old excuses. She didn't know what her life would be like without that old habit and she was afraid of it.

I talked a bit about fearing a future that can't possibly be predicted—another illusion of our own creation. Still I felt something more had to be revealed. I had to listen deeper still. Old familiar habits notwithstanding, what would make anyone afraid of a thing like freedom? The thought intrigued me. "Why would Julia be afraid of freedom?" I asked myself and again quieted my mind.

By this time we were back in the car beginning to drive away. We both saw it simultaneously.

Julia carried a deep-seated belief she didn't know she had: The reason she was afraid of freedom was because she did not believe she was worthy of being free.

That was big.

For nearly her entire life Julia felt bad about herself because of her thinking about how she'd been treated in her past and all the pain she'd been through. While now coming out of it she still felt unworthy. That was why she had all those stomachaches.

This new realization touched Julia deeply. There may even be deeper "whys" to explore—but for now it was enough for her.

There are always deeper and deeper levels of listening—to others and to ourselves. To deeply listen to ourselves is to be in a state of quiet reflection. We can ask ourselves a question, such as, "I'd like to see why I'm feeling stuck about this." Then forget it, put it out of our minds, quiet ourselves, go about our business and see what comes

X. We're only as stuck as we think we are

Alyson and her teenage son, Mark, were stuck.

They both showed up at a training I conducted on Maui. They knew I had written *Parenting from the Heart* and thought I might be able to help with an issue of great concern to both of them.

Mark had recently turned sixteen and got his driver's license. His parents gave him a car. They told him not to speed. He said he wouldn't. It took only a few months for Mark to be involved in five speeding incidents, one resulting in a blown tire on a lava-rock road.

This was unacceptable. Mark's father wanted to yank the car away from him forever. Alyson, the mother, thought this was too harsh; she wanted to put her foot down but was afraid of alienating Mark. Mark knew some kind of discipline was in order but feared what might happen. Both badly wanted a satisfactory resolution. Both were stuck. Both wanted me to address this incident. The other training participants agreed. They were curious about how I would handle a situation like this.

I had already talked with them about the three principles—Mind, Consciousness and Thought—and both Alyson and Mark had found it interesting. Our rapport felt right. So I questioned them and listened deeply. It was apparent they had an excellent relationship for a mother and teenage son.

Alyson said, as a consequence she was thinking of not allowing him to attend a summer musical play he was involved in. Mark desperately wanted to be part of this play.

I became puzzled. If the issue was the car and speeding, what did a summer play have to do with it? If I couldn't follow the logic I was pretty sure Mark couldn't. To me it only confused the matter.

I was also puzzled by Mark's behavior. I asked him if he knew what the expectations were for driving and having this car, and he said yes. Something didn't compute.

"This is curious," I said. "I'm wondering why someone who knows the expectations would violate those expectations?"

Mark said. "I don't mean to. There were just these situations..."

"So violating the expectations is okay, given certain situations?"

"Well, no, but..."

I let him ponder that a moment and turned to his mother. "Alyson, what is it that bothers you most about his behavior?"

She thought a moment. "Well, two things, really. First, if he's not going to be responsible, driving a car is really too dangerous. He could kill himself if he speeds."

I stopped her and turned to Mark. "Can you understand that from her perspective?"

He said, "Yes."

I turned back to Alyson. "What's the second thing?"

"This is the way it is all the time with Mark. I mean, I know he means well and he's a great kid, but often I have to tell him many, many times before he'll pick up anything that I ask him, or if he'll feed the dog, or things like that, and sometimes it doesn't even get done."

This interested me too. I said, "Well, if you have to tell him many times to do things it sounds to me that he doesn't think you're serious. So why should he think you're serious about the speeding? He doesn't have to comply as long as he doesn't think you're serious."

Alyson looked sheepish. The corners of Mark's mouth betrayed a tiny smile.

I turned to Mark. "Mark, you've told me you know what the expectations are, so what's on your mind when you speed?"

"I don't mean to. It's just that I forget."

Alyson chimed in. "Yes, he's so totally involved in whatever he's doing that he just forgets to do what he's asked—not just about the car but with many things, as I said."

"So the problem, then, really isn't the speeding. The real problem is 'forgets.' Speeding is a symptom of 'forgets.' But because speeding is such a dangerous symptom, you really need confidence that he's not going to speed, despite the fact that he forgets, right?"

"Absolutely."

I turned to Mark. "You can understand why a parent would need confidence that if you're going to be riding around in a lethal missile, she needs confidence that you're going to be safe, can't you?"

"Yes, I understand that."

"So, Alyson, this absolutely needs to be solved to your satisfaction because it's so dangerous. But in trying to solve it, if it doesn't get at the underlying issue of 'forgets' it's not going to work, see?"

"That's true, so what am I supposed to do? I know he's not doing it on purpose, but I can't be worrying that he's going to be in danger. What would you do?"

"What I would do isn't important."

"But I would really like to know what you would do."

I sighed. "Well, I would want my wisdom to speak to me. Knowing he's not doing it on purpose but knowing it's too dangerous to continue on like this, if it were me I would wipe the slate clean as of this moment and start fresh. But I would make it very clear that if he violates the speeding or car safety agreement even once more, good-bye car, period, no questions asked. If he knows that up front, then it's his decision what to do."

"Yes, that's great. That makes it real clear, and it's not too harsh because he's been given this new chance."

"But Alyson, if he did speed you'd absolutely have to follow through, you know? Otherwise this could go right back to the old pattern of thinking by letting him off the hook. Because you would feel bad about having to follow through and really take the car away from him, right?"

"I know."

Mark said, "That's fair."

I said, "Mark, if I were you I wouldn't be so quick to agree with this. I mean, there's a lot riding on it, literally, because if you violate this rule, no more car. I mean, what if you forget? We still haven't done anything about the issue of 'forgets.'

"No, I could do this."

125

"I'm not sure you'll be able to, honestly. I've noticed the speed limit is really low here on Maui. One little forgetful moment and it's all over, and you have a habit of forgetting. So I'm curious: What goes through your mind when you're asked to do something, before you forget?"

Mark reflected a moment. "I'm really involved in something, and I say to myself, 'Okay, just a minute until I finish up what I'm doing.'"

"And then?"

"I get involved again and don't think about it any more."

"Okay, so that's your habit. I can see how you're not doing this on purpose. But the fact is, what you're supposed to be doing isn't getting done. What about when you're driving?"

"Like I said, that's only when a special circumstance comes up, like if I'm running late or something."

Alyson chimed in. "He's late and leaves at the last minute because he gets so involved in what he's doing that he forgets to leave in time."

"Mark, so that's an excuse to speed?"

Mark said, "Well, I don't want to be late."

"So besides 'forgets,' the problem is also 'exceptions.'"

Sheepishly, he said, "Yes."

"Okay, remember what I said before about Thought creating our experience? In this case you're getting a double dose. Not only are you using your incredible gift of Thought to tell yourself, 'It's more important to finish what I'm into than do what I'm told right now,' and 'It's better to speed than to be late'—see, both of those thoughts give you a 'real' experience in your Consciousness that looks like it's truth—but on top of that, those thoughts *lead you* to behaviors that end up getting you in trouble."

Mark said, "Oh, that's what you meant before when you said it's an illusion."

"Yes, your thinking is tricking you, and you're falling for it, and it's leading you to the point where you're about to lose your car. And it's all started by believing those thoughts that pop into your head. But you don't have to! That's your protection. Because if you don't believe, 'I can just put off what I have to do for a moment' or 'I'm late so I'd better go faster'—if you allow thoughts like that to come in but then pass right on out—they can't do you any harm. And what will be left is listening to your own wisdom, which is telling you the best thing to do. That's your gut feeling telling you what's right. So you're going to have to be careful about believing that thinking, because it will end up with you losing your car. You see that?"

"I do. I won't speed if I don't pay attention to what those thoughts are telling me."

"Right! But right now you've got a habit of that kind of thinking, so you're definitely going to have those thoughts. That's what you'll want to keep an eye on: the thinking that, for example, is behind putting your foot down on the accelerator, or the thinking making you not want to leave a video game."

"Okay."

"And you, Alyson, are being tricked by your thinking, too. Do you know what you're being tricked by?"

"The thinking behind why I let him off the hook. I know what that is, too. I don't want him to have to suffer. I love him and I don't want him to be in any pain, and I don't want to hurt our relationship."

"It's also an illusion that taking a firm stand is going to hurt your relationship. In fact, in the long run it's really appreciated because it teaches him an important lesson."

They both agreed.

Now both were unstuck. What didn't look possible to either of them when they walked in apparently was possible after all. They thanked me profusely and left feeling satisfied.

When we feel stuck, we're not.

"Stuck" is another illusion. We're only stuck at the level of consciousness we can see at the moment. Why? Because it's all we can see! Of course we're stuck if it's all we can see. But it's only all we can see because we're looking from a fixed, narrow perspective. We can't see what's at a higher level of consciousness—yet! Whatever is up there brings other possibilities and hope. Our only limitation is what we see with our thinking in the moment.

While visiting the secluded, stunningly beautiful and peaceful Luna Lodge, nestled between the beach and rainforest in southwest Costa Rica, a guide named Oscar took a few of us on a hike to a waterfall. It was a short but steep downhill walk through the rainforest. I was about to wade into the pool at the bottom of the waterfall when Oscar said firmly, "Wait!"

He said an iguana had just scooted into the pool as we were walking in. No one but Oscar saw it. He said he'd try to get it out with a stick. Was he joking? I noticed he wasn't wading in there to get it, though, so I wasn't about to test it.

According to Oscar, usually mild-mannered iguanas that feel cornered or frightened can give a nasty bite. For about five minutes Oscar kept working the water with his walking stick. It sure looked as if there was nothing in there. Didn't iguanas need to come up for air?

Suddenly we saw a long tail appear from under the surface and go back down. Gulp! Apparently he wasn't kidding. Then a nose came up and disappeared again. For five more minutes he worked the water with his stick. Out it came, zipped back in, Oscar got it out again, and it scooted in again. Finally the iguana exhausted itself enough for Oscar to grab it by the tail. He set it on a rock. It could barely move from exhaustion. Now we could wade in.

The point is no one else saw it, and had we hiked down there and simply jumped in we could have been bitten badly. Suddenly I didn't trust any Costa Rican waterfall pools. Oscar assured us that iguanas never go into water unless trying to get away from something trying to eat them, such as a puma or a jaguar, which is why the iguana would have bitten us. That was comforting.

Nevertheless, I couldn't believe how often Oscar saw things we didn't—monkeys, birds, bats, spiders, plants, trees and flowers of all kinds—that he pointed out to us. His senses were acute in this jungle. We couldn't see what he saw. He was operating on a much higher level of consciousness than we and therefore saw much more. Because he saw more he could take action on what he saw. We couldn't.

Did that mean the same possibilities did not exist for us? No! It means from our limited perspective we couldn't see all the possibilities. We are always seeing from a more limited perspective than we could be. Although it's hard to imagine, maybe some people can see even more in the jungle than Oscar. Certainly jaguars can.

Auto mechanics see things about cars I would never see. When it comes to cars, they function at a much higher level of consciousness. Yet, as the "Car Talk" guys on National Public Radio illustrate regularly, top mechanics often see things other mechanics don't. But some top mechanics may not, for example, hear subtle variations within a classical music score. Musicians may not see the subtleties in paintings. Artists may not see the subtleties of science. Scientists may not see the subtleties that healers do. Healers may not see the subtleties within the strategy of a basketball game. About certain things everyone sees and functions at a fairly high level of consciousness, but in the rest of their lives they may not. In some cases the rest of their lives might be a mess. In those areas they function at low levels of consciousness. Yet in any area everyone is capable of seeing from a higher perspective than they do now.

When it comes to grasping or understanding or realizing the power of Universal Mind in our lives we are all amateurs. Even gurus, swamis, shamans and the great thinkers of the world throughout history have only caught what amounts to a glimpse compared with all that can be known. Yet the glimpse they have seen has allowed them to function at a much higher level than most of the rest of us. Infinite possibilities abound and await us.

When we have a problem we can't solve we're seeing at a lower level of consciousness than possible. We prove this again and again because later we often see a solution we didn't see before. We can look back at a problem in our past, which we couldn't resolve then, and now it's resolved. Or we say, "If I had only seen then what I see now!" Well, at that time we couldn't see more. We were limited by the level of consciousness—meaning, level of thinking—we saw then. Other possibilities still existed at other levels but we didn't know it because we were limited by our level of the moment.

This limitation is always illusion. We may not be able to see the illusion at the time. We don't know when we will see it. It may happen tomorrow, it may happen when we're 86, it may happen in the next moment. We have no idea. But at some other time we can almost guarantee the issue will look different. Simply to know we are never stuck is comforting. When we even acknowledge that there exist other levels we move to a higher level than a moment ago—because it feels more comforting.

In an interview in the documentary movie, *Don't Look Back*, Bob Dylan said (something like), "Look, we're all going to die. We're going to go off the face of this earth, and the world is going to go on without us. How seriously you take yourself in light of that, you decide for yourself." Wisdom! All forms eventually turn to dust. They're gone. Over time they disintegrate and are no more. In a million years will the pyramids in Egypt still exist? Two million? Maybe not, and they're probably the most powerful and lasting human-made structures presently on earth. Yet we take ourselves so seriously.

Maria walked into the middle of an ongoing, open-ended three principles/Health Realization drop-in group more overwhelmed than Gabriela had ever seen. She was crying, sobbing, moaning over and over, "I know I'm just going to die. I cannot live without him." She howled and talked intensely, incessantly, a mile a minute for forty-five minutes. She talked so fast Gabriela couldn't get a word in even to interrupt. She had just learned her husband was having an affair.

Maria wailed, "I'm sick. I'm sick!"

Maria looked it. She was not taking care of herself. Gabriela said Maria's breasts were practically hanging out of her torn blouse. She was a mess, inside and out.

"I'm diseased because my husband is an alcoholic and he has a disease," Maria cried. "I'm sick and my children are sick mentally because we've all been affected. I'm addicted to my husband. Without him I'm going to die. My three year old girl is being impacted. How can I do this to my children? But how can I stay with this man who is sick? I'm going to kill myself. That's the only way out."

Gabriela listened deeply. She felt for her. She waited for Maria to calm down some.

"Well, let's make a deal," said Gabriela, finally. "I'm going to say something to you, and would you be willing to trust me, even if you can't see what I'm talking about?"

"Yes," Maria whimpered.

Gabriela talked with her about innate Health. During her little talk Maria faded in and out; sometimes present, sometimes not. Whenever she faded Gabriela said, "Are you with me? Okay?"

"Okay, I'm ready again." Maria would kind of snap to attention, then begin to fade again.

The group ended for the day. Maria left. Gabriela had no idea if she would ever see her again. Maria returned the next week or so, calmer but still pretty intense.

"I'm trying to move out," she said. "My mind is sick," Maria kept repeating. "I have this disease. My children are sick mentally."

This time Gabriela talked with her about the three principles, how our experience is created from our own thinking.

"In spite of what you're going through," said Gabriela, "your Health is there, and you're using the principles to create a feeling of no health."

"But I'm sick. I'm sick."

Gabriela saw an opening. She said with a smile, "If you tell me you're sick one more time, you're going to owe me a tamale."

Maria looked startled, then laughed.

Gabriela continued: "I just want you to notice your Health for this week. Do we have a deal?"

"Yes."

"See you next time."

Two or three weeks passed before Maria showed up again. This time she seemed less intense. She no longer said, "I'm sick." She still didn't have a great feeling about her, but this was progress.

"I have to leave early because I have to pick up my son," she said, "but I want you to know I've started to discover myself, and I'm falling in love with my children."

A few more weeks passed before she came for a fourth session. She looked better. She wore a dress, heels and makeup.

"I've found a new apartment," she said. "I took myself and my kids away from my husband. I know he's doing the best he can, but I just had to leave. He deserves to have a nice life, but I do too. I am blessed to have my job, my children, myself. I looked in the mirror and saw how pretty I am. I'm starting to take care of myself. I'm beginning to discover how beautiful I am."

Gabriela said, "Sometimes when there's a problem situation you just have to wait—stay still and wait until wisdom talks to you, because otherwise you're a mess."

"Yes, I was a mess. I got depressed."

"It's letting your wisdom come through. Like when you're cooking rice you have to let it do what it does in its time. If you get in and stir it it makes a mess because you're getting in the way of the natural process."

Maria laughed. "Every time I start imagining all these bad things in my mind I will imagine the rice. If I get in my own way I'm drowning myself in water."

Gabriela smiled.

Maria left, saying, "I really need to be in my job now, so I don't know if I'll come next week."

Two weeks later she showed up, beaming. Maria now seemed the embodiment of well-being—the opposite of the chaos and despair she had displayed at first. This time she practically taught the class. She worked as a nurse at a convalescent hospital and talked of well-being and being of service to others.

"What I do is just be present with the person I'm caring for," she said. "I care for them and talk to them from my heart. Sometimes I tell God, 'This person can no longer be here,' and I say, 'It's time to take him,' and I tell them they can let go now. I tell them I love them, and then they die, and I say, 'Thank you, God.'"

She continued, "I'm just so in love with my children now, and I see how healthy and intelligent and loving they are. I tell them, 'You're beautiful! You're going to be just fine.' I've even been losing weight. I admire my face, and I'm just falling in love with myself. I drive my car, I have my job. I'm going to be just fine. Sometimes I experience low moods," she said, "but it's okay."

In this class Maria became teacher and had everyone in tears.

Gabriela witnessed this transformation before her very eyes. This was the same woman who'd been convinced she and her children were marked forever and doomed with a disease. Then Maria heard something about innate Health and the three principles, and she gained faith in life. To Gabriela this was a miracle. No one could have predicted it. It means there is hope for everyone.

None of us ever knows how long it will take for someone to change, or when it will happen. When we see complete despair and depression, someone overwhelmed by problems, some even committing horrendous acts, we often don't realize the possibility for a change of view, a change of heart. We often create limitations for people by what we see. We give up on people, write them off, which can limit their growth. Yet the possibility exists that anyone can change.

Gabriela asked Maria, "How did you change so quickly? How did you do this?"

Maria grinned, "I didn't want to lose the tamale."

Gab laughed.

"No, not really," Maria continued. "When I made that deal with you of seeing my Health instead of my disease, that was very, very helpful."

Even when we feel doomed, we're not. It's simply a creation of the mind.

Rewind. Gabriela's mother died an alcoholic. For ten years she had tried to convince her mother to put down the bottle, to get help, to do anything to help free her. Her mother didn't listen, and not because she didn't want to. She desperately wanted to. She thought herself a terrible mother because of this; it was not fair to her daughter, whom she loved so very much. But she couldn't break loose from the clutches of alcohol.

For so many years Gabriela lived with this frustration. She watched her mother deteriorate before her eyes. She loved her mother deeply, yet every interaction became strained. Gabriela tried to get her mother to act; her mother wouldn't budge. It pained her to be in the presence of her own mother! Yet nothing she could say or do would work. She found herself no longer wanting to even visit her because it was too frustrating, too painful. She felt terribly guilty about that.

Gabriela felt stuck—until the day she realized: if no matter what she did to try to get her mother to change was futile, if she did not want to have this frustrating relationship with her mother, if she deeply loved her mother and wanted the relationship to get back to the love it had always been, would it not make sense for the relationship to manifest that love? The only way this could happen was if Gabriela stopped trying to change her mother and instead showed her the love she truly felt for her.

The next time she saw her mother Gabriela said, "I realize that for all these years I've been trying to change you, to make you better. That has put a great wedge between us. I just want you to know I will no longer do that. I want you to know that no matter what you do I will always love you, and when I am with you from now on I just want to spend nice time with you."

Her mother felt eternally grateful. She loved her daughter so. She felt so guilty and weak.

From that moment on Gabriela and her mother regained their wonderful relationship. Everything came unstuck. Gabriela never knew whether she did the right thing, but nothing she had tried before had worked, and now she had three wonderful, loving years visiting her until her mother finally died of alcoholism.

Gabriela only knew it felt right.

What do we know about what we're here for? What is our purpose in life? What if the situations we feel stuck about are for the purpose of new learning? What if we are being put through it all for the purpose of moving to a new level of understanding in life? We don't really know if this is true, but this possibility exists. If we did see it that way, though, we wouldn't be so bummed out or fearful about whatever we are going through. Instead we would be curious and open to what we don't yet see. Who decides which way we see it?

Moving to increasingly higher levels of consciousness is like climbing a tall tower. The higher we go the more we can see. On lower levels we see only what immediately surrounds us; on higher levels we see the entire panorama. On lower levels we have limited perspective; at higher levels we see with greater perspective. On higher levels we see our way out of "lostness." We only feel stuck at lower levels because at that time we can't see the higher levels. On higher levels we look down at our lower level self and see how far off we were. On lower levels we don't know what's on the higher levels because we can't see what it looks like from up there. But we can know with certainty that something better is in store for us up there, even if we can't yet see it.

We could get laid off at work and be freaked out about it, only to have another, better opportunity come around that we would have missed had we stayed at our initial job. When running late for an appointment we could be cursing behind a driver going at a snail's pace, only to drive by a policeman waiting around the next corner with a radar gun. We never know the future! At higher levels there is always new hope. If we knew this we would no longer feel stuck.

One winter in college my daughter, Jaime, was hurrying across campus. She slipped on ice and fell down a set of concrete stairs, landing hard on her coccyx. It hurt so badly she could barely move. They took her to the Infirmary and she ended up in the Emergency Room. She had so much to do and now couldn't do it. She lay in great pain, bemoaning her fate. While there, a doctor noticed some swelling in her neck, unrelated to the fall. Turned out she had a horribly infected abscessed tooth she didn't know about. The doctor said if it hadn't been caught that very day the infection would have burst and gone up into her brain. If she hadn't fallen down the stairs she may have lost her life, or at least the quality of it.

What looks like horror in one moment could be a blessing in the next. We never know!

If Mind is All things, everything we see on earth and beyond is all part of the One. Yet we think we're stuck with our own little thoughts. Doesn't it seem like something greater than ourselves exists, some mysterious force in the universe that we can't see? Some people call it a higher power, some people call it the Creator, the Great Spirit, some call it Master Mind; some call it pure energy, the life force, some call it God—people call it all kinds of things. The name isn't important. What is important is *Knowing* that no matter how bad things look, because we're all part of this One pure essence there really is nowhere to fall. We are a tiny part of this essence. We cannot be separate from the One; it is impossible! It only looks as if we're separate. Our separateness is an illusion.

I certainly live a lot of my life forgetting I'm part of the Oneness of Mind—until I remember in moments. During those times I think I'm separate it feels as if I really am and I become fearful. But it's only my own self-created illusion of fear. This is the duality of life. We can only *think* separateness; we cannot *be* separate. We see separateness only because we have thoughts that we're separate. Even if we don't consciously think such thoughts it is what we see. But to realize the Allness, to see the greater, to see the Oneness, is to know that all the petty garbage we think up and experience is awfully pathetic compared with that. In the grand scheme of things there is nothing to fear. All we need is faith.

But how can we have faith when we don't have faith? How can we have faith when we may not believe It even exists? I don't have an answer. All I can say is the answer is probably in front of our eyes, only we're too busy dismissing as a fluke the moments we connect with this essence. We write off those moments as unreal.

On two or three occasions in my life, out of nowhere, I remember *seeing* everything in perfect order. Everything suddenly looked perfect, even autumn leaves scattered seemingly randomly on the grass, even garbage seemingly strewn aimlessly. In those moments I *saw* absolute perfection; I saw an order to it all. This felt huge. It hit me hard—then it was gone. I could no longer see what I saw moments before, no matter how hard I tried. I could easily have dismissed that as a fluke, chalked it up to my mind playing tricks on me. Many people do. But I didn't because I *saw* something I recognized as *Truth*. I couldn't even question whether it was true. I *Knew*.

Here's the kicker: even if I'm wrong, knowing this made me feel better. It felt comforting for me to know this. That's good enough for me.

If we don't have faith it is easy to stay fearful. Or we could test it out: Simply have faith and see if it all works out in the end. I learned that from my daughter, Jaime.

From George Pransky I learned that having faith does not mean something will work out for us the way we want; having faith means *we will be okay no matter how it works out*.

Often I forget this is true. I forget all is in perfect order. I forget it's all a perfect unfolding, no matter what happens. But once in a while I remember, and when I do I feel comfort again. I feel a deep richness about life. Because I know "stuck" is an illusion. *We're only as stuck as we think we are.* That's a mind-blowing statement, at least to me.

Megin's life and work had been helped greatly from attending a long-term professional Three Principles training. Yet, one time she told me how painful it was for her to have to clean her house. She lived with and took care of her elderly, infirmed father. For most of her life she despised housecleaning and saw it as a huge chore. So when she did have to do it, she did it grumbling and in low spirits. As I listened to her it occurred to me that all life is a series of moments, moments strung together like a string of pearls. The moment appears, then it's gone, and a new moment appears. We get to make of each moment what we will. A moment of housecleaning can either be a joyful moment or a distressing moment. We could be thrilled with the prospect of making something clean. We could use it as a time of meditation. Who decides? We do—from how we've made it up for ourselves. It can happen equally in a housecleaning moment or in any moment. .

Each moment in life is as beautiful as we see it, and the way we see it can always change. We think we're stuck, then we have new thought, then what we saw as a pain in the neck or a problem or a dead end suddenly looks different.

Our lives are lived in our heads.

All life is a continual change of thought, a continual stream of thought flowing through, changing, changing, changing. It only appears to be static in the moment, then we realize it's changed again. That's the other secret to never being stuck: Knowing *our thinking will change and with it our experience will change*. One of the most important things we can know about life is that it's never coming from out there. It's always us, us, us!

We're always going to forget. There isn't a soul on earth who doesn't feel stuck from time to time. Nobody I know is so good they can stay in the present moment all the time. Everybody has low states of mind from time to time. Everybody gets caught in their thinking habits. That seems to be the human condition. At times everyone thinks there is no way out.

Sometimes we get stuck in double binds where it seems any way we turn is a problem. Our protection lies in understanding how life works, knowing we are only limited by what we can see now. We don't have to believe that the bind we see in the moment is all there is. The Oneness doesn't care if we believe it or not; whether we believe it or not we're still part of the essence. There is nothing we can do about it—except forget.

And if we forget for a while, so what?

Teresa's Story

Teresa attended a forty-five hour "Health Realization and Its Application in School Settings" course that I taught during the school year for staff at the Thatcher Brook Primary School in Vermont. Below is the final paper she submitted. I asked her if I could use it for this book.

When I began this class, I thought I was taking a class that would "teach" me to be healthy. For weeks, almost months into the class I still thought that Jack could teach me how to behave healthy. Then almost in an instant, that "teaching" became intrinsic. I felt it in my heart, my soul, and my mind. I found "GRACE." The dictionary gives one definition: a virtue coming from God. This is the definition with which I choose to relate. Looking back over my life, I have gone through many mini-revelations and had many life-altering experiences. However, it wasn't until the past seven months, while taking this class and attending a weekly Bible study that it all came into perfect view for me.

As a little girl I was born to an alcoholic father and a very young, sad, mother. Only weeks after my little brother was born, my mother found my father with another man. At 1½ years old, me, my infant brother and my mother moved far away and had no contact with my biological father for many, many years. Soon after, my mother met another alcoholic who had four children from a previous marriage. As you can imagine, many horrible things did happen, including physical, emotional and sexual abuse to me.

At 15 years old, after confronting my mother with the news about the sexual abuse that she was unaware of or chose not to notice, I decided to move out of my home and live with friends until I graduated from high school. I did very well in school, despite the circumstances of my life. Something kept me going. Something from inside, a place I couldn't articulate, but I had hopes and dreams and wasn't going to let anything stop me.

I applied to only one college: Trinity College, a small, all-girls school in Burlington, Vermont. I wanted to work with children and families, for sure! Why? Looking back, I know why! It's all part of the plan for me.

Within those crazy 17 years I questioned life. I had "why me?" pity-parties. I started to indulge in alcohol, sex, shopping, etc., etc., etc.

Then, at 19 years old, almost my junior year in college, I got married. At 20 I had my first child. Still finishing school, working and raising my baby, I gave birth to my second child, still with my hopes and dreams high. I will be a teacher! Something was pushing me from inside! At 22 I graduated college, ready to conquer the world. What I hadn't noticed is that I already had.

At 24, I gave birth to my third and final baby, Trevor. At three months old he died of SIDS. Something helped me through this tough time. I could have chose (without knowing it was a choice) to go into depression, to take medicine to deal with the guilt. What did I do wrong? I knew, looking back, that according to studies, he was dressed too warm. He was lying on his belly. He had too many blankets, etc., etc., etc. But, something (me) let it go. I took my sadness and created opportunity to share my knowledge with others. We had car washes for 5 years after his death, raising money for the SIDS Institute and awareness in the community. However, it wasn't without many set-backs.

During those five years I changed jobs often, was so close to divorce, claimed bankruptcy, was a terribly grumpy mother to my living children. Guilt, shame, sadness, anger, blame, jealousy, hatred, greed, spite all clouded my life. Then, I was invited to church by a friend. I thought, why not? Maybe all this can help me. That was two years ago. I started to learn that life wasn't all about me. Bad things happen to good people, it's what we do when they happen that defines where we are and where we will go, knowing that no matter what's happened in our lives, what choices we've made, today, this minute, this second is a new beginning.

Then, a year and a half after seeking a relationship with God, I began taking this class. That's when it all came together for me. I am the only person who controls how I feel. If I choose to feel happy, sad, angry, guilty, etc. it is me who is controlling those emotions. It is that simple. The things that have happened in my life in the past have happened. I cannot change these things. They are my past. I must accept them or if I choose, I can deal with them in my head and drive "myself" crazy. I can believe that people have set out to hurt me, to ruin me, I am supposed to be sad, depressed, I deserve this, etc. but I will not! Which brings me to my next point: The Serenity Prayer.

Lord, help me to accept the things I cannot change,
The courage to change the things I can,
And the *wisdom* to know the difference.

Since this class I have allowed my wisdom to let me truly accept the things I can not change which means to forgive my mother, my step-father, my father, husband, my children, friends, my family, my co-workers, for the things I once thought they were doing to hurt me, that I now realize they did because they weren't in their health. I realize these things that happened in my life can only hurt or bother me if I choose to let them. Sometimes I do choose to let others behaviors bother me. However, I see the power my forgiveness and unconditional love can bring to others.

I believe that life is bigger than each of us. I believe that we all have a purpose. I believe that our wisdom will help us find that purpose. I believe that we should forgive ourselves and others the way God is willing to forgive us. I believe we should do our best to abide by the golden rule, "Do unto others as you'd have done to you." I believe that if we can do these things, we can live life the way God intended, and in my mind this is "Health Realization." We aren't perfect, we don't always behave in the most healthy ways, but if we forgive ourselves and others we will always see our health!

Amen!

Thank you, Jack for helping me see my health and understand "who" gave me my wisdom.

Jack Pransky

XI. Putting it All Together

While on the road one day I learned that a woman named Margaret from Pittsburgh, whom I didn't know, had placed a desperate call to me. Apparently she had been referred by her daughter's friend who'd had similar problems but was helped immeasurably by a three principles practitioner in Minnesota, so she thought I might be able to help her, too.

"I'm desperate," she said.

I asked what her problem was.

She blurted out that she was horribly depressed and had recently been released from a mental institution where she'd committed herself after being suicidal and now she was on what seemed an okay dosage of medication but she was barely able to get by especially when she went to visit her mother whom she visited every other day because her mother tortured her when she was a child and she desperately wanted to be free of medication like her daughter's friend now was and to live a normal life. Whew! I don't think she took a breath.

I told her my fee and that I didn't know whether I could help her.

She said, "Unfortunately, I'd never be able to afford that because I'm on disability."

She sounded *so* depressed.

I said, "Okay, look, I don't believe anyone should be denied services because of money, so I would be willing to speak with you now for free—one time—if you give me five minutes and call me back."

She said that would be wonderful.

I dropped what I was doing, took a deep breath, got focused, and she called. She began by telling me a terribly tragic story about her past. She was convinced her mother always hated her; in fact her mother told her this many times. Now her mother was 85 years old—

Margaret was 60—and Margaret kept going over there to take care of her mother who apparently continued to torture her. Margaret felt horrible about herself.

I cut her off. I had a flash that if I was only going to speak with her once I had to teach her *the three principles* and let the chips fall where they may.

JP: Wait a second, Margaret, are you saying you think your mother and what she did to you in the past is the reason you're feeling depressed today?

M: Yes.

JP: And that's the reason you've felt suicidal, and the reason you had to check yourself into a mental institution?

M: Yes—and somewhat my father too. He used to treat me badly too. They used to fight horribly all the time.

JP: Well, I can understand why you would think that, because of how you were treated when you were growing up and how your mother treats you still, but the thing you most need to understand is that isn't true.

M: [stopped in her tracks] What do you mean?

JP: I mean to think that is to give up all your power.

M: I'm convinced what happened to me is the cause of all my problems.

JP: I know, and as long as you think that you're stuck with it.

M: I've been to many, many psychotherapists and psychiatrists, and they think so, too.

JP: And everything you've thought and everything they've thought has gotten you where you are today.

M: [quiet] I guess so. But I don't understand what you're saying.

JP: Okay, look, what I do is help people understand where their experience of life comes from and how they function as human beings, and that seems to help a lot of people. Would you be interested in that?

M: If you think that will help me, yes.

JP: But I want to warn you that I'm not going to guarantee that this one session will help you. I'm especially not saying you're going to get off medication. I don't even recommend that you try to get off medication. If you ever get ready to do that you'll likely know when that will be because your body will start feeling like it's ready. Do you still want to continue?

M: Yes.

JP: Okay, the thing I want you to do first, right now, is take all your problems and the past off your mind. I want you to empty your mind. I want you to have a clear mind when you listen to this, okay? I just want you to get a feeling from what I'm going to say and just take it in without thinking too much about the words. Just pick up the feeling of it, okay?

M: Okay.

JP: I'm going to talk about Three Principles, and when I say "Principle" I'm not talking about a theory, but I mean "Principle" as a force in the universe that exists whether we know about it or not. It's kind of like gravity exists in the natural world. Before people knew gravity existed they were still being held to the earth. So that's the level I'm talking about. I'm saying, just like gravity is a principle of the natural world, there are three principles of the psychological/spiritual world. Are you following me?

M: Yes.

JP: First let me ask you a question, okay?

M: Sure.

JP: You told me you were feeling different now than when you were suicidal, and different than when you checked yourself into the mental hospital, right? Why do you think that is?

M: [reflected for a moment] Maybe it's because I'm not quite as dependent on my mother as I was.

JP: I thought you said that you see her every other day and she still tortures you.

M: Yes, that's true, she does. But it used to be every moment, and now it's not that constant. [pause] Well, I guess maybe it's because I'm on medication.

JP: So what's different now that you're on medication?

M: [started to go into a long story about the difference in her mother now, but I cut her off.]

JP: Margaret, I mean in general, not the specifics.

M: I guess I don't know.

JP: Would you say your thinking is different than it was when you were suicidal?

M: Yes.

JP: And that's giving you a different feeling?

M: Yes.

JP: And when you see your mother do you always come away with the exact same feelings?

M: Well, no, sometimes these days she actually tells me she appreciates something I've done. So when she does that I feel pretty good. But then she'll wipe me out again.

JP: Nevertheless, you sometimes feel differently than you usually do.

M: Yes.

JP: What's changed? I don't mean what your mother does. I mean in you.

M. I guess sometimes it's not on my mind as much as it is at other times.

JP: Exactly! And would you say that what's on your mind is different when you're feeling suicidal, compared with the way you're feeling now?

M: Yes.

JP: That's the first two principles.

M: What?

JP: That we're blessed with this incredible gift. We have this awesome power of creation. We get to create any thoughts we want. We even create thoughts we don't think we want, but we create them just the same. God knows where some of these thoughts come from, but one thing for sure, they come from us. We're the ones who think them. Are you with me so far?

M: Yes.

JP: And you told me your feelings were different, right? That's the second principle. Besides the incredible power of Thought, we have also been blessed with the incredible gift of Consciousness. Without consciousness we would have no experience of life. Consciousness is our power to experience life. If we were unconscious we wouldn't have any experience, right?

M: True.

JP: Now listen to this: Every time we think a thought it comes back to us in the form of an experience. When you're with your mother, what do you usually come away thinking?

M: That she makes my life miserable.

JP: And how are you feeling at that time?

M: Miserable and depressed.

JP: That's exactly what I mean.

M: But she does make me miserable!

JP: She does whatever behaviors she does. She says whatever she says to you. Then you take your creative power of Thought and you *think* that what she does affects you and makes you miserable. So then you get an experience of misery—a feeling of misery and depression.

M: Well, how else am I supposed to feel?

JP: I'm not saying you should be feeling any way. I'm saying that whatever you're thinking about what she does to you is what you're getting.

M: I'm confused. Her behavior is miserable and nasty toward me. Are you saying it isn't?

JP: I'm saying it's just behavior. If you think it's miserable and nasty, then it is—to you. Then you get that as an experience in the form of your feeling. I'm saying no one can possibly make you miserable—except you! If you weren't thinking miserable thoughts when you think of her and what she does to you, you wouldn't feel miserable. I mean if, for example, you ever felt sorry for her for living such a miserable life that she feels she has to take it out on you, then you'd get a different experience. You wouldn't feel miserable, you'd feel something else, like compassion.

M: I have felt that at times. But it's rare.

JP: But it happened! If it happened even once, it happened, and you had a different feeling because you happened to be having different thoughts. What I'm talking about here, Margaret, is your freedom. You've given up all your power to her since you were very young, and you're still doing it. I mean, who's the one choosing to go over to her house and see her and take all the abuse?

M: [sheepishly] I am.

JP: That's your own thinking. You hand yourself over to her on a silver platter and say, "Here, make me miserable." And she obliges. Then you think, "See, she always does this to me. I can't escape it." Then you get a miserable feeling. It's foolproof!

M: Oh my God!

JP: What?

M: Have I really been the one doing that—all these years? That's almost too much to take.

JP: That's what you've been doing. But you're not alone. Most of us believe we're being affected by the outside world. Also, it's not your fault. That's what you saw. You couldn't help it. You couldn't see any more than you could see. And, want to know something else?

M: What?

JP: Neither could your mother. She could only see what she could see. Her thinking led her to see you in a certain way, therefore feel a certain way, therefore act toward you in a certain way. Just like you, she was doing the best she could do, given the way she saw things.

M: Whew. I'm kind of blown away. I don't know what to think right now.

JP: You don't have to know. It's good to not know. That means anything is possible. Don't forget, if you look closely at your thinking you can see it changes, and with it your experience changes. You told me you didn't always feel the same way. That's because your thinking shifted. Our thinking is constantly changing, and with every new thought we get a new experience. Like right now you're baffled. I'm guessing you're not miserable right at this moment, are you?

M: No, at this moment I'm not.

JP: But you were when you called. See? Different thinking, different experience, different feelings. Doesn't it make you wonder how seriously we should take any particular experience we're having in the moment? When a new thought comes along, that experience will change. We might not be able to make a new thought come along and change our experience right now, but eventually we will get a different thought—guaranteed. If we know a different thought will come and eventually give us a different experience, why would we want to hang on to any one lousy experience and make it be our life?

M: [almost sighs] So I'm supposed to change my thinking?

JP: Well, no, wait a minute. Do you have control over whatever thoughts you think?

M: Are you saying I should?

JP: No, I'm not. We already said we don't go out of our way to think most of the thoughts that come into our head. We have no control over most of that. We only have control over one thing.

M: What's that?

JP: What we make of what comes into our head. How seriously we take the thought. How much we let it get to us. Whether we take it to heart or let it pass through without getting to us. How much we let it have meaning for our life.

M: Like what?

JP: Like when I get a thought, "I'm stupid," which happens from time to time, I don't believe it.

M: That happens to me all the time. But I believe it. My mother always told me that, and I started to believe it.

JP: That's what I'm saying. The only difference is, I get that thought and I don't believe it—I don't really think I'm stupid, so I don't have that experience. You get the thought, you believe it, and you feel stupid. Whether we believe our thinking or not is up to us. Another thought either reinforces the first thought or overrides it. That's all we have control over. You have no control over what your mother says to you or what thoughts come to mind about it, only how you take it. As I said, you've been giving your power over to your mother when you're the one in charge of the experience you're getting.

M: Ohhhh! I see.

JP: And we haven't even talked about the third principle: Where do our gifts of the power of Thought and the power of Consciousness come from? They have to come from somewhere. They don't belong to us alone. They are universal powers. They come from what we call Universal Mind. The intelligence behind life. The energy behind life. Some life force that allows us to be alive and is much greater than we are works through us and gives us those powers. Lucky us, we're not left to the devices of our own thinking. If we weren't thinking, that life force, that energy, that spirit would still be flowing through us.

M: Are you talking about God?

JP: Well, I might call It that, except people's interpretations or conceptualizations of what God is can be pretty narrow.

M: I know. I still see a Catholic God who is very judgmental of me. I think God must have punished me for something. I keep asking Him to free me from this but He hasn't listened.

JP: How do you know He hasn't listened? Maybe He sent you to me, for all you know. But that's why I like to call it Mind, instead, because all our conceptions together are much too limiting. It's much greater than any of that. All I know is it's a force within us and everything else and we're just a tiny little part of it, but it gives us automatic Health and love and well-being and peace of mind. And if it were possible to have no thoughts (which it probably isn't, but we can come a lot closer than we do), that's what we would be. We can tell because when our mind clears or calms down, that's what we experience. So without our thinking, that's what and who we *really* are! The only thing that can possibly get in the way is our own thinking. We can only think ourselves away from this pure, uncontaminated state. Only *we* can contaminate it, and we do that with our own thinking, therefore we get a contaminated experience. But that's an illusion, too. We can't really be separate from it, because It is all there is. It never goes away. *What you are searching for, you already have!* It's just like the sun behind the clouds. Even in a huge snowstorm you have absolute faith the sun is still there, even though you can't see it in the moment. And when the storm and clouds pass, it's there again for you to see. But it never went anywhere, did it? The clouds only make it look as if it isn't there, and we get fooled by that. But it's always there. Always. Always. And it's the same in us. That beautiful part of us—all of us—is like the sun, and it's always there for us, even when it looks like it isn't.

M: Wow, what you said to me then—of all the things you said to me—I really felt that. I've been looking so much to have hope. I've never had hope. But this gives me hope for the first time.

JP: Yes, if our spirit can never be destroyed and our pure spirit— our soul—has these qualities and reveals itself to us when our negative thinking or our busy thinking stops—like the clouds moving on out—that's automatic hope.

M: Yes, I see that now. Oh my God, I can't believe I've been doing this to myself. I can't believe what I've been doing to myself all these years.

JP: Yeah, it can be kind of humbling. But you could use your power of Thought to beat yourself up for that, too.

M: [laughs]

JP: And that would be thinking that gives you a down experience and blocks the pure spirit of Mind from coming through.

M: Wow, I can't believe nobody ever told me this before. I can't believe how many psychologists and psychiatrists I've had who just wanted me to dig deeper into my problems. I thought that's what I had to do.

JP: When you have a bruise, do you go poking at it to heal it?* Or do you allow the natural healing process to heal from within? The same natural healing process occurs with our so-called psychological problems and traumas. We will get thoughts about the trauma, but if we don't make something of those thoughts—if we just allow them to pass through, feel whatever we feel about them but let them pass on through—then they can't do us harm, and over time the thoughts will get lighter and will have less of a grip over us. Right now they've had you by the throat, but that's only because you're letting those traumatic feelings say to you, "This is what my life is. This is who I am." You're making that up. It's an illusion.

M: Wow! That makes so much sense. Those psychologists and psychiatrists just wanted me to dig deeper into the pain, and it never helped me. I never seemed to get anywhere. I feel like I've gotten farther in this session than I have in all the years I've gone to them combined.

JP: But the world of psychology is innocent, too. They don't know this—yet. They've been trained to look at the underlying problems. A lot of them hear this and they think it's crazy. Some of them even get insulted. They say, "It can't be that simple! People and their problems

---

* Another George Pransky metaphor. Thanks again, George.

are more complex than that." But it *is* that simple. The only thing that makes human beings complex is the creative content of their thinking. Some psychologists even say what we're teaching is dangerous. Yet it seems to help so many people. I don't know what they make of that. Maybe they think we're fooling people or tricking them into feeling well.

M: I think this will make a big difference for me.

JP: One last thing, because I think you've had enough for today, but I just had the flash that I should read you a small section from a book I wrote, because it's a conversation with a woman named Lisa whose situation had similarities to yours. [I read the following:]

> Lisa: My mother [stepmother] treated me like dirt. She hated me.
> JP: So let me get this straight, your mother went out of her way to treat you badly?
> L: Yes.
> JP: She wanted to hurt you?
> L: Yes.
> JP: So, like, she woke up each morning and said, "What can I do to hurt Lisa today?"
> L: Hmm.
> JP: When it comes right down to it, how do you know what was on her mind about you?
> L: It was like I was in her way.
> JP: How do you know?
> L: That was the way she acted toward me. I couldn't do anything right! She told me I couldn't wash clothes because I would break the washing machine. I couldn't peel potatoes because I would waste too much of the potato. I've lived my whole life with that.
> JP: But, do you know what was behind it?
> L: What do you mean?
> JP: I mean, what was her motive for saying things like that to you?"
> L: I don't know.
> JP: Wait a minute, you told me she deliberately wanted to hurt you. Isn't that what you're saying her motive was?

L: I guess, well—

JP: So you go around making up her motive, and then you get to suffer the consequences of what you made up.

L: Hmm.

JP: Okay, okay, let's say the absolute worst is true. Let's say that she really did get up every day and say, "How can I hurt Lisa today?"—which I doubt, but let's say she did—do you think she knew what she was doing?

L: What do you mean?

JP: Could she have helped it, given her thinking?

L: I don't know—I mean, No—I don't—[great sorrow overcame her]

JP: I truly feel for you. It must have been so hard growing up with that. But can you see her innocence? And what about yours? Picture yourself as a little baby crying in your crib, and your mother can't stand it. Could you have helped it? Could you have done anything differently?

L: [sighing deeply, clutching her heart] I feel like I've got this deep pain in my heart.

JP: I'm so sorry. What are you seeing now?

L: [All of a sudden, something went whoosh] Oh my God! I just saw myself for the first time! It was like part of me was behind me, facing the other way, and I could never see her, and suddenly, Oh my God, I just turned around and saw myself for the first time! I just looked at myself, and I realized that I blamed myself for everything. I feel so sorry to have done that. I'll never see myself in the same way again. Just like with Bridgett, I'll never see myself in the same way again.

Out in the parking lot, as Lisa was leaving...[she] said, "Goodbye, I'm going back to my hotel room..." Then she stopped, turned around, looked at me and, with astonishment, said, "...with myself!" She came running back to me, and said, "Oh my God, Jack! I'm never going to be alone again! I finally have myself!"

M: Wow, that really meant a lot to me. I could relate so much. Thank you so much!

JP: You could be free, like Lisa is. It's not that she still doesn't have those old thoughts popping into her head, because they're such ingrained habits, but she's free because she knows she doesn't have to take them to heart and let them rule her. And she's free because she knows when she doesn't let that thinking get to her and it departs she really is a Healthy, wise human being. And she is. And so are you.

M: Thank you so much. I am so grateful. I can't believe nobody told me this before.

It all looks so simple to me now—until I forget in some moments, then remember again. Essence is simplicity. This is what truly empowers us: To see that the Creator has endowed us with certain inalienable gifts, and we get to use these gifts in whatever way we want. We decide what we give power to, whether consciously or not.

To sum it all up:

1) We have been given *the gift of the power of creation*, the gift that with our power of Thought we can create anything within our own minds. This is an awesome, incredible gift: the power of creation— *Thought*.

2) We have been given *the gift of the power to experience* whatever our thoughts create and to be aware of Thought and how it works and how we're using it in any moment. This is the gift of *Consciousness*. We have the power to see the thinking and the resultant feelings we create as "reality" or illusion. That's power!

3) We have been given *a source of healthy creation*. *Mind* is All things and gives us All, yet the pure essence and Oneness of Mind comes through us as our spiritual essence, our Soul. Whatever one calls it, it contains automatic peace of mind, automatic well-being, automatic Health, automatic wisdom. Thus, along with the gifts to create anything and to experience whatever we create, we also have within us an automatic source of healthy creation. We do not have to do anything to get it for it is already present in us always. This wellspring nourishes us. All we can do is allow it to flow freely in us or get in its way (with our own thinking).

We have also been given *a pathway to healthy creation*. This pathway is a clear mind. All we need is for our typical, everyday thinking to shut down. When this happens, our Health/wisdom automatically appears—because it never went anywhere. The clouds part, the sky clears, the sun comes out. It was there all along.

We have also been given *the means to continuously self-monitor our creations: Our feelings and emotions.* As a self-monitoring mechanism they are foolproof. Feelings such as well-being, love, compassion, humility, humor and gratefulness tell us we're close to our Health and wisdom. Low or fearful or worried or angry emotions tell us our thinking is off track and can't be trusted. We may not be aware of what we're thinking, or even that we're thinking, but we could always be aware of what our feelings are telling us, and make adjustments.

Life is levels of consciousness. Sometimes we're up; sometimes we're down. But only one thing can make us be up or down: the way we *use* our creative gift of Thought. And that is what we experience within our consciousness. This is the simplicity. If we weren't thinking any thoughts all that would be left is our pure essence that gives us everything we ever need. Some levels are closer to the pure essence of Mind than others. We have the free will to create Health or misery, peace or war, happiness or sorrow, love or hate. We use our creative power of Thought to decide which we accept for ourselves, and then our consciousness gives us the experience of whatever we create.

The more we allow life to flow through us instead of using our thinking against ourselves, the more our lives will embody peace, love and well-being. Nearly everyone I know would like more of that in their lives, along with healthy relationships and less stress. How do we get there? Through understanding how it all really works. In my experience, everything I've said in this book can be boiled down to two things:

1) People will increase their well-being to the extent they understand that their problems, difficulties and stress *never* come from the outside world but only from how they use their thinking.

2) People will increase their well-being and peace of mind to the extent that they allow themselves to be guided from a clear mind by their Health and wisdom.

The more we realize our experience comes from within us, the more what we seek in life appears in our lives. The more we see illusions of our own creation as opposed to "reality," the less we are controlled by the illusions we inadvertently create and get to live with. The more we allow our wisdom to guide us instead of our typical personal or analytical or habitual or low mood thinking, the more we stay on track of our Health and do not go astray.

That doesn't seem so difficult, does it?

We have the ability to see limitation or see infinite possibilities. It's all up to us.

What a gift!

And it's yours. It's mine. It's everyone's.

I don't know about you, but I'd sure like to use it for my own peace of mind, and for the peace of the world, than against myself or others.

The End, And a New Beginning

Final Summary

1. Our thinking is our life.

2. Wisdom is always available to guide us, if we know how to access it.

3. If someone's thinking doesn't change, they can't change.

4. When our mind clears our wisdom appears.

5. We don't have to think our way out of our problems (or to happiness).

6. The feeling is what counts, and it's foolproof.

7. What we see is what we get.

8. In low levels of consciousness it is unwise to believe, trust or follow our thinking.

9. To deeply listen to others instead of to our own thinking gives us a richer experience

10. We're only as stuck as we think we are.

- -

For further information, please go to Jack Pransky's website: www.healthrealize.com.

Also see *Three Principles Global Community, Inc.* www.3PGC.org.

READER REVIEWS

I found Jack's book *Somebody Should Have Told Us!* to be the most life-changing piece of work I've come across. I've been reading self-help material for the past twenty years and none of it has had a lasting effect. Having read this book twice in the last few months, my life has changed completely, and without much effort...The most thrilling aspect of what Jack teaches is that life really is easy until our thoughts get in the way of our natural wisdom... I recommend you throw away all your self-help books and buy this wonderful piece of work. It gently informs us that change comes from within and trying to learn external techniques will never work... I can't write enough good things about this book and I feel so grateful it's come into my life.

Brian Hill
Rochester, UK

This book has given me much hope! It is written with such honesty and wisdom that you can't possibly walk away from it without being touched in some way... I would encourage *everyone* to experience his approach...I personally have "let go" of so much heartache that has had control of me for most of my life. This understanding also helped me to realize that after being *miserable* for 10 years from the loss of my mother, I could live again...[and] be happy. You want to read [it] over and over again. Each time you may have a new insight and see more of yourself. I am currently going through one of the most difficult and challenging times of my life and this book gives me a tremendous amount of comfort! I will be ok, no, I will be *spectacular*!... Thank you... It has the ability to change our world!

Karen Olson-Thomas
Topeka, KS

Health Realization [*the three principles*] has brought me the deepest sense of serenity I have ever experienced. It has allowed me to use the innate power I have always known existed and believed in but never knew how to harness it and use it to its infinite potential. I have learned and fully accepted that "*I create my reality*" and that by living in this light- I can make anything happen and can choose to react to everything in a manner which keeps me in my own personal health. I possess everything I need within me, as each of us does- and that is truly empowering.

Alicia Walmsley
Chicago, IL

Unsolicited praise for Jack Pransky's book, *Prevention from the Inside-Out*:

Reading your book has helped me understand my life. The thing that is amazing is that while reading it -- it seemed as if you were telling me something I already knew somewhere inside of myself. I could "feel" the truth of it with absolute certainty. As if this knowledge had simply been lying dormant, waiting for a spark to ignite it. Now I know the only thing wrong with me is my Thought about what is wrong with me and I can choose to think differently about myself, just as I chose to think differently about getting out of bed or getting angry. I have the thought that this "understanding" cannot be happening this fast. Then again I have been searching 40 some years for some kind of understanding to happen, and how long can an insight take? It seems the epiphanies are rolling through my head as I type...

Barbara, Topeka, KS

Unsolicited praise for Jack Pransky's book, *Parenting from the Heart*:

This book saved my life—and it probably saved my kids' lives too.

Gail, St. Johnsbury, VT

Praise for Jack Pransky's book, *Modello: A Story of Hope for the Inner City and Beyond*:

Modello is a compelling, inspiring and true story of what is possible when people learn to access their inner wisdom and human potential through an understanding of *The Three Principles*. *Modello* shows us unequivocally that when people are armed with even a glimpse of the power and promise of *The Principles*, their self-esteem, well-being and common sense can rise to levels that enable them to transform even the most dire circumstances. In this book, Jack Pransky - one of the very best of the *Three Principles* authors - gives us an invaluable gift that is a beacon for a troubled world. He articulates clearly the "inside-out" approach used at Modello, and shows us how it touches one person - one heart - at a time until these simple truths produce profound change. After reading his true account of the miracle at Modello, the reader is compelled to imagine the infinite possibilities that exist for this approach in our families, communities, schools, hospitals, jails, government agencies and businesses.

Don Donovan, Business Executive

CPSIA information can be obtained
at www.ICGtesting.com
Printed in the USA
BVHW072316060919
557677BV00002B/180/P